POPE FRANCIS

Care for Creation

POPE FRANCIS

Care for Creation

A Call for Ecological Conversion

Edited by Giuliano Vigini

ORBIS BOOKS
Maryknoll, New York 10545

ORBIS BOOKS
Maryknoll, New York 10545

Fathers and Brothers
MARYKNOLL™

Founded in 1970, Orbis Books endeavors to publish works that enlighten the mind, nourish the spirit, and challenge the conscience. The publishing arm of the Maryknoll Fathers and Brothers, Orbis seeks to explore the global dimensions of the Christian faith and mission, to invite dialogue with diverse cultures and religious traditions, and to serve the cause of reconciliation and peace. The books published reflect the views of their authors and do not represent the official position of the Maryknoll Society. To learn more about Maryknoll and Orbis Books, please visit our website at www.maryknollsociety.org.

Library of Congress Cataloging-in-Publication

Names: Francis, Pope, 1936- author. | Vigini, Giuliano, 1946- editor.
Title: Care for creation : a call for ecological conversion / Pope Francis ;
   edited by Giuliano Vigini.
Description: English edition. | Maryknoll, NY : Orbis Books, [2016] |
   Translation of: Custodire il creato : proposte per una conversione
   ecologica. | Collection of some of Pope Francis' writings on the
   environment.
Identifiers: LCCN 2016006851 (print) | LCCN 2016007193 (ebook) | ISBN
   9781626981898 (pbk.) | ISBN 9781608336593 (ebook)
Subjects: LCSH: Human ecology—Religious aspects—Catholic Church. |
   Ecology—Religious aspects—Catholic Church. | Environmental
   protection—Religious aspects—Catholic Church. | Environmentalism—Moral
   and ethical aspects. | Environmental justice—Religious aspects—Catholic
   Church. | Ecotheology.
Classification: LCC BX1795.H82 F73 2016 (print) | LCC BX1795.H82 (ebook) |
   DDC 261.8/8—dc23
LC record available at http://lccn.loc.gov/2016006851

Contents

Introduction   ix

CHAPTER 1

Care for Creation   1

The Gift of Creation   1
Human Ecology   2
Cultivating and Caring   3
Taking Care of Creation   5
Caring for One Another   6
The Future of the World's Garden   8
Fulfilling a Plan of Love   9
The Supreme Good of Life   11
Creation, Gift of Peace for All   12

CHAPTER 2

Degrading Our Common Home   14

Irreversible Damage to the Ecosystem   14
The Climate under Threat   15
The Abuse and Destruction of the Environment   16

Contents

The Human Environment and the Natural Environment   18
The Relation between Nature and Society   19
The Deterioration of Institutions   20
The Distortion of Technology   21
The Poor, Victims of Environmental Degradation   22

CHAPTER 3
Ethical Failure   24

A Time of Permanent Inequality   24
The Scandal of Hunger   25
Hunger for Dignity   28
The Idolatry of Profits   29
A Culture of Encounter   31
Unacceptable Waste   33
Imbalance in Consumption   34

CHAPTER 4
This Economy Kills   36

An Economy of Exclusion   36
The Invisible Tyranny   38
The Fetishism of Money   41
The Distortion of the Marketplace   42
Ensuring Economic Freedom   43
Money Must Serve, Not Rule   44
An Economy at the Service of the People   45
An Honest Economy   48
Solidarity   49
Inequality, the Root of Social Ills   51

Contents

CHAPTER 5

The Globalization of Indifference   53

Insensibility to the Suffering of the Other   53
The World of the Excluded   54
Abandoned to the Laws of Economy   55
The Cry of the Poor   55
The Cry of the Earth   57
The Spread of Inequality   58
Cultivating Justice   59
The Temptation of a False Peace   61

CHAPTER 6

Redefining Progress   62

We Need a Change   62
Process of Change   64
For a Better World   65
Looking for Progress in a New Way   66
Interaction between the State and the People   67
Far-sighted Politics   68

CHAPTER 7

The Search for the Common Good   70

The Principle of the Common Good   70
Welfare and the Common Good   71
Building Bridges   73
The Earth and the Common Good   75
Working for the Rights of All   75
Thinking about Future Generations   77

Contents

CHAPTER 8

Toward a Culture of Integral Ecology   79

Defending Mother Earth   79
A Far-reaching Vision   80
Ecological Education   81
Lifestyles for Changing the World   84
Ecological Conversion   87

CHAPTER 9

Constructing the Human City   90

God Lives in Our Cities   90
The Defense of Dignity   93
Serving the Person, Not the Ideology   94
Touching Human Misery   96
Poverty Teaches Solidarity   97
The Responsibility of Believers   98
We Need Each Other   99
Universal Fraternity   99

CHAPTER 10

The Spiritual Dimension of Life   102

The World at Risk   102
Quality of Life   103
Sharing with Others   103
Welcoming Others   104
Healing Fundamental Relationships   105
Keeping Hope Alive   106
A Revolution of Tenderness   109

Introduction

GIULIANO VIGINI

Pope Francis has made a big impression as a "personality" by his unpretentious and familiar style of talking, and especially by his ability to communicate effectively in a direct and intense way. But beyond these more "superficial" aspects, he has made his mark in these early years of his papacy by the radical nature of his decisions for the Church and in pastoral matters. These have undoubtedly begun a new era in the Church's life. Of course, as well as the disarmingly ordinary way in which he speaks and behaves, his charisma, sympathy, friendliness, and fatherly warmth have done much to shape the "outward" presence of the man who became pope and immediately divested himself of his "sacral" authority.

There are the risk that Francis's great popularity might remain merely superficial, only playing on feelings and with no more than an immediate emotional appeal. But, as the months went by, he went deeper, and his winning personality also communicated the freshness of his gospel message to people's hearts. His choice of the name Francis (as a program for his life and apostolic mission), moving as he did to the Casa Santa Marta, and his morning Mass homilies for small groups clearly signaled substantial changes. Today we can see more clearly the full scope of these changes and this pope's way of understanding and carrying out the office of "bishop of Rome." We realize that these early gestures were only the beginning; gradually we have seen the growth of Francis's dominant idea of a church called as the "people of God" to go out of herself toward the margins, to find the poorest (in both material and existential terms), the excluded, the rejects of society. And on so many occasions Francis himself has given an example by means of particular actions, displaying a strong sense of each person's uniqueness and dignity.

At the same time Francis has proceeded with unusual speed and determination in his efforts to reform the structures of the Curia. Throughout this process he has repeatedly stressed that no reform can bear fruit if it is not accompanied by inner renewal of the individuals concerned and their total commitment to serve. But, above all, the pope's attention has been concentrated on people's problems—which he encounters more and more often in Italy and throughout the world. (His pastoral visits and apostolic trips have been more numerous and far-reaching than was initially anticipated.) He has focused on the urgent needs of a world beset by terrorism, war, and poverty. He has led the Church in making great efforts to foster international relations, quite often playing an acknowledged, important role in mediation. He has also intensified inter-religious and cultural dialogue.

This is the wider context in which to set the question of caring for creation, the theme addressed by Francis in *Laudato Si'*, the encyclical released in 2015. Its impact was enormous, reflecting the importance and urgency of its subject. Pope Francis wanted to make believers and all those of good will aware of the present precarious state of the planet. His powerful message was to restore the Earth as a beautiful home for a loving family that can offer a future of justice and peace for all.

The key question running throughout the document is this: How must we act, politically and economically, ethically and spiritually, to correct the mis-development that not only threatens to spoil the Earth but also to impoverish and degrade the human beings living on it? Here it would be reductionist to consider the encyclical merely as a detailed analysis of ecological problems and possible remedies to be adopted nationally or by individuals. In fact, *Laudato Si'* is more like a manifesto for a new humanism. Even its title, invoking the opening words of St. Francis's *Canticle of the Creatures*, sums up the spirit that should move its readers: all who care for the fate of creation and want to live responsibly on Earth, cultivating and caring for it with respect and common kindness as a gift of God's love.

This is what Francis offers us, a global vision of humanity and the world, with multiple relationships and responsibilities enabling us to live together in our common home.

So the ecology the encyclical speaks about is not an end in itself; it is ecology for the sake of humanity. It is not just a tile in the mosaic but the mosaic of life itself, to be constructed for its own sake and for future generations. That is why the subject cannot be avoided. Francis's merit is to have treated it systematically, gathering many reflections and opinions, starting from the magisterium of his predecessors (particularly John Paul II and Benedict XVI, whom he often quotes). He also refers to the Orthodox tradition, documents of bishops' conferences from various countries, and numerous expert studies.

From Vatican II onward, the Church has declared ever more vigorously that a fundamental starting point for reflection on creation is that Earth's riches belong to us all and so should be fairly distributed. There should be no imbalance and all people should be enabled to provide a decent living for themselves. But the scandal is that exactly the opposite occurs. The lust for power and greed for money prevail, causing exploitation and exclusion, the dominance of a senseless form of politics, a blind economic imperialism, uncontrolled financial speculation, and excessive consumerism that promotes what John Paul II called "market idolatry."

In this situation the quality of the environment and life—the one being closely connected to the other—is seriously damaged, and there is a breakdown in the moral order that alone can guarantee fairness in the use of natural resources, peaceful co-existence between human beings, and the physical and spiritual well-being of all. Clearly, if there is not a determined fight against everything that degrades the Earth and debases human beings at the very heart of governments' thoughts and actions and the behavior of individuals, we cannot recover the bond wedding us to nature in wisdom and harmony.

This means that the ecological challenge demands first and foremost a complete change of ethical course and a change in education to support it. Development can be sustainable for today and tomorrow only if it derives from "human ecology," which is concerned with taking care of the whole human being and all human beings in their full dignity as persons. Hence it indirectly also improves the natural environment in which each person is set, so that common interests may prevail over the privileges of the few. Such an approach to development supports and conserves both the natural and human environment. It promotes and defends life from birth to death. It builds connecting bridges rather than dividing walls between nations. That is the human ecology which helps preserve the garden of the world in which God has set humanity.

In recent years the Church has stressed with increasing concern the theme of poverty and the existing gap between rich and poor on the planet: hunger, lack of water, pollution, waste, climate change, desertification, loss of biodiversity, soil erosion, deforestation...The Church has stood guard over a wide-ranging reflection on the ethical, cultural, and educational roots of the environmental problem.

It has not offered technical solutions, which are beyond its domain, but it has worked to raise awareness, so that people realize or rediscover the fundamental values by which to "re-plan" the environment and society. Indeed, for the Church the urgent ecological problem is first and foremost an educational emergency. We must become fully conscious of the need to educate ourselves and others to live in a new way in the world as it really is. Divine and human values must come together to rediscover the meaning and age-old insights of Christian doctrine, ethics, and anthropology.

As this collection of texts shows, even before *Laudato Si'* Pope Francis addressed the subject of care for creation on a number of occasions. He has denounced the things that are wrong with our system and the consequences this had led to. He has been outspoken and direct on poverty and injustice, degradation and waste, the globalization of indifference that is deaf to the groans of humanity and the Earth. But now his encyclical is an indictment calling upon our individual and collective responsibility to take reasonable care of the natural resources that belong to all, and that must be distributed and used for the benefit of all. The encyclical is a true compendium of Christian social doctrine, which sets out the priorities for an "ecological conversion" and a genuinely "integral ecology": unity against fragmentation; a systematic approach against any partial, separate, or exclusively scientific-technical perspective; dialogue and collaboration between states and governments against any form of ideological conflict or the temptation to make unilateral decisions; constant effort to renew links between individuals and nations against any withdrawal into a "private and particular" scenario. That is without forgetting what each one of us, as a Christian and a human being, can do to improve and progress in truth and goodness. This is the humanism that Francis is lucidly portraying as a project of civilization for our common home, and the task to which he calls each one of us.

—Translated by Dinah Livingstone

1

Care for Creation

THE GIFT OF CREATION

In the gospel we have just heard, Jesus, the Master, teaches the crowds and the small group of his disciples by accommodating himself to their ability to understand. He does this with parables, like that of the sower (cf. Lk 8:4–15). The Lord is always flexible in his way of teaching. He does it in a way that everyone can understand. Jesus does not seek to "play the professor." Instead, he seeks to reach people's hearts, their understanding and their lives, so that they may bear fruit.

The parable of the sower speaks to us of "cultivating." It speaks of various kinds of soil, ways of sowing and bearing fruit, and how they are all related. Ever since the time of Genesis, God has quietly urged us to "cultivate and care for the earth."

God does not only give us life: he gives us the Earth, he gives us all of creation. He does not only give man a partner and endless possibilities: he also gives human beings a task, he gives them a mission. He invites them to be a part of his creative work and he says: "Cultivate it! I am giving you seeds, soil, water, and sun. I am giving you your hands and those of your brothers and sisters. There it is—it is yours. It is a gift, a present, an offering. It is not something that can be bought or acquired. It precedes us and it will be there long after us.

—*Meeting with Educators, Pontifical Catholic University of Ecuador,*
Quito, July 7, 2015

HUMAN ECOLOGY

When we talk about the environment, about creation, my thoughts go to the first pages of the Bible, to the book of Genesis, where it says that God puts men and women on the earth to till it and keep it (cf. 2:15). And these questions occur to me: What does cultivating and preserving the earth mean? Are we truly cultivating and caring for creation? Or are we exploiting and neglecting it? The verb "cultivate" reminds me of the care a farmer takes to ensure that his land will be productive and that his produce will be shared.

What great attention, enthusiasm, and dedication! Cultivating and caring for creation is an instruction of God which he gave not only at the beginning of history but has also given to each one of us. It is part of his plan. It means making the world increase with responsibility, transforming it so that it may be a garden, an inhabitable place for us all. Moreover, on various occasions Benedict XVI has recalled that this task entrusted to us by God the Creator requires us to grasp the pace and the logic of creation. Instead we are often guided by the pride of dominating, possessing, manipulating, and exploiting; we do not "preserve" the earth, we do not respect it, we do not consider it as a freely given gift to look after.

We are losing our attitude of wonder, of contemplation, of listening to creation and thus we no longer manage to interpret in it what Benedict XVI calls "the rhythm of the love story between God and man." Why does this happen? Why do we think and live horizontally? We have drifted away from God, we no longer read his signs.

However "cultivating and caring" do not only entail the relationship between us and the environment, between man and creation. They also concern human relations. The popes have spoken of a *human ecology*, closely connected with *environmental ecology*. We are living in a time of crisis. We see it in the environment, but above all we see it in men and women. The human person is in danger: this much is certain—the human person is in danger today, hence the urgent need for human ecology!

—*General Audience, June 5, 2013*

CULTIVATING AND CARING

Our world is a gift given to us by God so that, with him, we can make it our own. God did not will creation for himself, so he could see himself reflected in it. On the contrary: creation is a gift to be shared. It is the space that God gives us to build up with one another, to build a "we." The world, history, all of time—this is the setting in which we build this "we" with God, with others, with the earth. This invitation is always present, more or less consciously in our life; it is always there.

But there is something else which is special. As Genesis recounts, after the word "cultivate," another word immediately follows: "care." Each explains the other. They go hand in hand. Those who do not cultivate do not care; those who do not care do not cultivate. We are not only invited to share in the work of creation and to cultivate it, to make it grow and to develop it. We are also invited to care for it, to protect it, to be its guardians. Nowadays we are increasingly aware of how important this is. It is no longer a mere recommendation, but rather a requirement, "because of the harm we have inflicted on [the earth] by our irresponsible use and abuse of the goods with which God has endowed her. We have come to see ourselves as her lords and masters, entitled to plunder her at will...This is why the earth herself, burdened and laid waste, is among the most abandoned and maltreated of our poor" (*Laudato Si'*, 2), that exist today in the world.

—*Meeting with Educators, Pontifical Catholic University of Ecuador,*
Quito, July 7, 2015

TAKING CARE OF CREATION

The vocation of being a "caretaker"... is not just something involving us Christians alone; it also has a prior dimension which is simply human, involving everyone. It means caring for all creation, the beauty of the created world, as the book of Genesis tells us and as Saint Francis of Assisi showed us. It means respecting each of God's creatures and respecting the environment in which we live. It means caring for people, showing loving concern for each and every person, especially children, the elderly, those in need who are often the last we think about. It means caring for one another in our families: husbands and wives first protect one another, and then, as parents, they care for their children, and children themselves, in time, protect their parents. It means building sincere friendships in which we protect one another in trust, respect, and goodness. In the end, everything has been entrusted to our protection, and all of us are responsible for it. Be caretakers of God's gifts!

Whenever human beings fail to live up to this responsibility, whenever we fail to care for creation and for our brothers and sisters, the way is opened to destruction and hearts are hardened. Tragically, in every period of history there are "Herods" who plot death, wreak havoc, and mar the countenance of men and women.

Please, I would like to ask all those who have positions of responsibility in economic, political, and social life, and all men and women of goodwill: let us be "caretakers" of creation, caretakers of God's plan inscribed in nature, protectors of one another and of the environment. Let us not allow omens of destruction and death to accompany the advance of this world! But to be "caretakers," we also have to keep watch over ourselves! Let us not forget that hatred, envy, and pride defile our lives! Being caretakers, then, also means keeping watch over our emotions, over our hearts, because they are the seat of good and evil intentions: intentions that build up and tear down! We must not be afraid of goodness or even tenderness!

—*Inaugural Homily, March 19, 2013*

CARING FOR ONE ANOTHER

"Adam, where are you?" This is the first question that God asks man after his sin. "Adam, where are you?" Adam lost his bearings, his place in creation, because he thought he could be powerful, able to control everything, to be God. Harmony was lost; man erred and this error occurs over and over again also in relationships with others. "The other" is no longer a brother or sister to be loved, but simply someone who disturbs my life and my comfort. God asks a second question: "Cain, where is your brother?" The illusion of being powerful, of being as great as God, even of being God himself, leads to a whole series of errors, a chain of death, even to the spilling of a brother's blood!

God's two questions echo even today, as forcefully as ever! How many of us, myself included, have lost our bearings? We are no longer attentive to the world in which we live; we don't care; we don't protect what God created for everyone, and we end up unable even to care for one another!...

"Adam, where are you?" "Where is your brother?" These are the two questions which God asks at the dawn of human history, which he also asks each man and woman in our own day, and which he also asks us. But I would like us to ask a third question: "Has any one of us wept because of this situation and others like it?" Has any one of us grieved for the death of these brothers and sisters? Has any one of us wept for these persons who were on the boat? For the young mothers carrying their babies? For these men who were looking for a means of supporting their families? We are a society that has forgotten how to weep, how to experience compassion—"suffering with" others: the globalization of indifference has taken from us the ability to weep! In the gospel we have heard the crying, the wailing, the great lamentation: "Rachel weeps for her children... because they are no more." Herod sowed death to protect his own comfort, his own soap bubble. And so it continues...Let us ask the Lord to remove the part of Herod that lurks in our hearts. Let us ask the Lord for the grace to weep over our indifference, to weep over the cruelty of our world, of our own hearts, and of all those who in anonymity make social and economic decisions that open the door to tragic situations like this. "Has any one wept?" Today has anyone wept in our world?

—*Homily at the Island of Lambedusa*
(a point of entry for immigrants, many of whom drown at sea), July 8, 2013

THE FUTURE OF THE WORLD'S GARDEN

We are not God. The earth was here before us and it has been given to us. This allows us to respond to the charge that Judeo-Christian thinking, on the basis of the Genesis account which grants man "dominion" over the earth (cf. Gen 1:28), has encouraged the unbridled exploitation of nature by painting him as domineering and destructive by nature. This is not a correct interpretation of the Bible as understood by the Church. Although it is true that we Christians have at times incorrectly interpreted the scriptures, nowadays we must forcefully reject the notion that our being created in God's image and given dominion over the earth justifies absolute domination over other creatures. The biblical texts are to be read in their context, with an appropriate hermeneutic, recognizing that they tell us to "till and keep" the garden of the world (cf. Gen 2:15). "Tilling" refers to cultivating, ploughing, or working, while "keeping" means caring, protecting, overseeing, and preserving. This implies a relationship of mutual responsibility between human beings and nature. Each community can take from the bounty of the earth whatever it needs for subsis-

tence, but it also has the duty to protect the earth and to ensure its fruitfulness for coming generations.

—Encyclical Laudato Si', *67, May 24, 2015*

FULFILLING A PLAN OF LOVE

The gift of knowledge sets us in profound *harmony with the
Creator* and allows us to participate in the clarity of his vision and his judgment. And it is in this perspective that we
manage to accept man and woman as the summit of creation, as the fulfillment of a plan of love that is impressed
on each one of us and that allows us to recognize one another as brothers and sisters.

All this is a source of serenity and peace and makes the
Christian a joyful witness of God, in the footsteps of St.
Francis of Assisi and so many saints who knew how to
praise and laud his love through the contemplation of creation. At the same time, however, the gift of knowledge
helps us not to fall into attitudes of excess or error. The first
[such error] lies in the risk of considering ourselves the
masters of creation. Creation is not some possession that we
can lord over for our own pleasure; nor, even less, is it the
property of only some people, the few. Creation is a gift, it
is the marvelous gift that God has given us, *so that we will
take care of it and harness it for the benefit of all, always with
great respect and gratitude.* The second erroneous attitude is
represented by the temptation to stop at creatures, as if

these could provide the answer to all our expectations. With the gift of knowledge, the Spirit helps us not to fall into this error.

But I would like to return to the first of these incorrect paths: tyranny over rather than the custody of creation. We must protect creation, for it is a gift which the Lord has given us, it is God's present to us. We are the guardians of creation. When we exploit creation, we destroy that sign of God's love. To destroy creation is to say to God: "I don't care." And this is not good: this is sin.

Custody of creation is precisely custody of God's gift and it is saying to God: "Thank you, I am the guardian of creation so as to make it progress, never to destroy your gift." This must be our attitude to creation: Guard it, for if we destroy creation, creation will destroy us! Don't forget that. Once I was in the countryside and I heard a saying from a simple person who had a great love for flowers and took care of them. He said to me: "We must take care of the beautiful things that God has given us! Creation is ours so that we can receive good things from it; not exploit it, but to protect it. *God forgives always, we men forgive sometimes, but creation never forgives and if you don't care for it, it will destroy you.*"

This should make us think and should make us ask the Holy Spirit for the gift of knowledge in order to understand better that creation is a most beautiful gift of God. He has done many good things for the thing that is most good: the human person.

—*General Audience, May 21, 2014*

THE SUPREME GOOD OF LIFE

The love of Christ urges us (cf. 2 Cor 5:14) to make our-selves the servants of the small ones and of the old, of every man and every woman whose primordial right to life is to be recognized and protected. The existence of the human person, to whom you dedicate your solicitude, is also your founding principle; it is life in its unfathomable depth which originates and accompanies all scientific progress; it is the miracle of life which always places in crisis any form of scientific presumption, restoring primacy to wonder and beauty. Thus Christ, who is the light of mankind and of the world, lights the way so that science may always be a knowledge at the service of life. When this light falters, when the knowledge forgets the contact with life, it be-comes infertile. For this reason, I invite you to keep your gaze fixed on the sacredness of each human person, so that science may truly be at the service of mankind, and not mankind at the service of science.

Using a magnifying glass, scientific reflection pauses to analyze certain details. Thanks to this analytical capacity too, we reaffirm that a just society recognizes as primary the right to life from conception to its natural end. I would like us, however, to go further, and to think carefully about the time that joins the beginning with the end. Therefore, in rec-ognizing the inestimable value of human life, we must also reflect on how we use it. Life is first and foremost a gift. But this reality generates hope and a future if it is enlivened by fruitful bonds, by familial and social relationships which open new prospects.

The level of progress in a society is measured by its capacity to safeguard life, above all in its most fragile stages, more than by the spread of technological instruments. When we speak of mankind, we must never forget the various attacks on the sacredness of human life. The plague of abortion is an attack on life. Allowing our brothers and sisters to die on boats in the Strait of Sicily is an attack on life. Dying on the job because the minimum safety standards are not respected is an attack on life. Death from malnutrition is an attack on life. So are terrorism, war, violence, euthanasia. Loving life means always taking care of the other, wanting the best for him, cultivating and respecting her transcendent dignity

— Address to participants in a meeting sponsored by
the Science and Life Association, May 30, 2015

CREATION, GIFT OF PEACE FOR ALL

We are going through World War III but in installments. There are economic systems that must make war in order to survive. Accordingly, arms are manufactured and sold and, with that, the balance sheets of economies that sacrifice man at the feet of the idol of money are clearly rendered healthy. And no thought is given to hungry children in refugee camps; no thought is given to the forcibly displaced; no thought is given to destroyed homes; no thought is given, finally, to so many destroyed lives. How much suffering, how much destruction, how much grief. Today, dear brothers and sisters, in all parts of the earth, in all nations, in every heart and in grassroots movements, the cry wells up for peace: War no more!

An economic system centered on the deity money also needs to plunder nature to sustain consumption at the frenetic level [that system] needs. Climate change, the loss of biodiversity, deforestation are already showing their devastating effects in terrible cataclysms which we see and from which you the humble suffer most—you who live near the coast in precarious dwellings, or are so economically vulnerable that you lose everything due to a natural disaster. Brothers and sisters, creation is not a possession that we can dispose of as we wish; much less is it the property of some, of only a few. Creation is a gift, it is a present, it is a marvelous gift given to us by God so that we might care for it and use it, always gratefully and always respectfully, for the benefit of everyone.

—Address to the World Meeting of Popular Movements,
Rome, October 28, 2014

2

Degrading Our Common Home

IRREVERSIBLE DAMAGE TO THE ECOSYSTEM

Time, my brothers and sisters, seems to be running out; we are not yet tearing one another apart, but we are tearing apart our common home. Today, the scientific community realizes what the poor have long told us: harm, perhaps irreversible harm, is being done to the ecosystem. The earth, entire peoples, and individual persons are being brutally punished. And behind all this pain, death, and destruction there is the stench of what Basil of Caesarea—one of the first theologians of the Church—called "the dung of the devil." An unfettered pursuit of money rules. This is the "dung of the devil." The service of the common good is left behind. Once capital becomes an idol and guides people's decisions, once greed for money presides over the entire socioeconomic system, it ruins society, it condemns and enslaves men and women, it destroys human fraternity, it sets people against one another and, as we clearly see, it even puts at risk our common home, sister and mother earth.

I do not need to go on describing the evil effects of this subtle dictatorship: you are well aware of them.

—Address to the second World Meeting of Popular Movements,
Santa Cruz de la Sierra, Bolivia, July 8, 2015

The Climate under Threat

The climate is a common good, and today it is under serious threat, as can be seen in phenomena such as climate change, global warming, and the increase of extreme weather events. These themes are the subject of great media attention and of public opinion, and are the focus of many heated scientific and political debates, from which has emerged widespread, though not yet unanimous, consensus.

How and why can we address it? We cannot forget the serious social implications of climate change, as it is the poorest of the poor who suffer the consequences with the most difficulty! Therefore, as the title of this meeting does well to highlight, the climate issue is a matter of justice and also a matter of solidarity, which can never be separated from justice. The dignity of each person is at stake, as a people, as a community, and as men and women.

Science and technology place an unprecedented power into our hands. We have a duty to all of humanity, and in particular to the poorest of the poor and to future generations, to use it for the common good. Will our generation "be remembered for having generously shouldered its grave responsibilities" (*Laudato Si'*, 165)? Even among the many contradictions of our time, we have sufficient grounds to nurture hope that it can be done. We must let ourselves be guided by this hope. In fulfilling this commitment, I hope that each of you may experience the delight of taking part in life-affirming actions. The joy of the gospel dwells here too.

In what way can we exercise our responsibility, our solidarity, and our dignity as people and citizens of this world? Everyone is called to respond personally, at the level of responsibility one has, based on the role one occupies in the family, in the workplace, in the economy and research, in civil society, and in institutions. Not by proposing improbable solutions: no one has them! Rather, by offering to the dialogue what they understand, and accepting that their contribution may be called into question. Everyone is asked to contribute toward a solution that can be the result only of a joint effort. The great enemy here is hypocrisy.

— Address to participants of a meeting sponsored by
the Foundation for Sustainable Development, September 11, 2015

The Abuse and Destruction of the Environment

It must be stated that a true "right of the environment" does exist, for two reasons. First, because we human beings are part of the environment. We live in communion with it, since the environment itself entails ethical limits that human activity must acknowledge and respect. Man, for all his remarkable gifts, which "are signs of a uniqueness which transcends the spheres of physics and biology" (*Laudato Si'*, 81), is at the same time a part of these spheres. He possesses a body shaped by physical, chemical, and biological elements, and can survive and develop only if the ecological environment is favorable. Any harm done to the environment, therefore, is harm done to humanity. Second, because every creature, particularly a living creature, has an intrinsic value, in its existence, its life, its beauty, and its interdependence with other creatures. We Christians, together with the other monotheistic religions, believe that the universe is the fruit of a loving decision by the Creator, who permits man respectfully to use creation for the good of his fellow men and for the glory of the Creator; he is not authorized to abuse it, much less to destroy it. In all religions, the environment is a fundamental good (cf. ibid.).

The misuse and destruction of the environment are also accompanied by a relentless process of exclusion. In effect, a selfish and boundless thirst for power and material prosperity leads both to the misuse of available natural resources and to the exclusion of the weak and disadvantaged, either because they are differently abled (handicapped), because they lack adequate information and technical expertise, or because they are incapable of decisive political action. Economic and social exclusion is a complete denial of human fraternity and a grave offense against human rights and the environment. The poorest are those who suffer most from such offenses, for three serious reasons: they are cast off by society, they are forced to live off what is discarded, and they suffer unjustly from the abuse of the environment. They are part of today's widespread and quietly growing "culture of waste."

The dramatic reality this whole situation of exclusion and inequality, with its evident effects, has led me, in union with the entire Christian people and many others, to take stock of my grave responsibility in this regard and to speak out, together with all those who are seeking urgently-needed and effective solutions. The adoption of the *2030 Agenda for Sustainable Development* at the World Summit, which opens today, is an important sign of hope. I am similarly confident that the Paris Conference on Climatic Change will secure fundamental and effective agreements.

—Address to the General Assembly of the United Nations,
New York, September 25, 2015

The Human Environment and the Natural Environment

There is a relationship between our life and that of Mother Earth, between the way we live and the gift we have received from God. "The human environment and the natural environment deteriorate together; we cannot adequately combat environmental degradation unless we attend to causes related to human and social degradation" (*Laudato Si'*, 48). Yet just as both can "deteriorate," we can also say that they can "support one another and can be changed for the better." This reciprocal relationship can lead to open-ness, transformation, and life, or to destruction and death.

One thing is certain: we can no longer turn our backs on reality, on our brothers and sisters, on Mother Earth. It is wrong to turn aside from what is happening all around us, as if certain situations did not exist or have nothing to do with our life. It is not right for us, nor is it even humane to get caught up in the play of a throwaway culture.

Again and again we sense the urgency of the question that God put to Cain, "Where is your brother?" But I won-der if our answer continues to be: "Am I my brother's keeper?" (Gen 4:9).

—Address to the Pontifical Catholic University of Ecuador,
Quito, July 7, 2015

THE RELATION BETWEEN NATURE AND SOCIETY

When we speak of the "environment," what we really mean is a relationship existing between nature and the so-ciety that lives in it. Nature cannot be regarded as some-thing separate from ourselves or as a mere setting in which we live. We are part of nature, included in it and thus in constant interaction with it. Recognizing the reasons why a given area is polluted requires a study of the workings of society, its economy, its behavior patterns, and the ways it grasps reality. Given the scale of change, it is no longer pos-sible to find a specific, discrete answer for each part of the problem. It is essential to seek comprehensive solutions that consider the interactions within natural systems themselves and with social systems. We are faced not with two separate crises, one environmental and the other social, but rather with one complex crisis that is both social and environmental. Strategies for a solution demand an integrated approach to combating poverty, restoring dignity to the excluded, and at the same time protecting nature.

—*Encyclical* Laudato Si', *139, May 24, 2015*

THE DETERIORATION OF INSTITUTIONS

If everything is related, then the health of a society's institutions has consequences for the environment and the quality of human life. "Every violation of solidarity and civic friendship harms the environment" (Benedict XVI, *Caritas in Veritate*). In this sense, social ecology is necessarily institutional and gradually extends to the whole of society, from the primary social group, the family, to the wider local, national, and international communities. Within each social stratum, and between them, institutions develop to regulate human relationships. Anything that weakens those institutions, such as injustice, violence and loss of freedom, has negative consequences. A number of countries have a relatively low level of institutional effectiveness, which results in greater problems for their people while benefiting those who profit from this situation. Whether in the administration of the state, the various levels of civil society, or relationships between individuals themselves, lack of respect for the law is becoming more common. Laws may be well framed yet remain a dead letter. Can we hope, then, that in such cases, legislation and regulations dealing with the environment will really prove effective? We know, for example, that countries which have clear legislation about the protection of forests continue to keep silent as they watch laws repeatedly being broken. Moreover, what takes place in any one area can have a direct or indirect influence on other areas. Thus, for example, drug use in affluent societies creates a continual and growing demand for products imported from poorer regions, where behavior is corrupted, lives are destroyed, and the environment continues to deteriorate.

—*Encyclical* Laudato Si', *142, May 24, 2015*

The Distortion of Technology

It can be said that many problems of today's world stem from the tendency, at times unconscious, to make the method and aims of science and technology an epistemological paradigm which shapes the lives of individuals and the workings of society. The effects of imposing this model on reality as a whole, human and social, are seen in the deterioration of the environment, but this is just one sign of a reductionism which affects every aspect of human and social life. We have to accept that technological products are not neutral, for they create a framework that ends up conditioning lifestyles and shaping social possibilities along the lines dictated by the interests of certain powerful groups. Decisions that may seem purely instrumental are in reality decisions about the kind of society we want to build.

—*Encyclical* Laudato Si', 107, May 24, 2015

THE POOR, VICTIMS OF ENVIRONMENTAL DEGRADATION

I would like to focus on three principles. First of all, the principle of solidarity, a word that is sometimes forgotten and at other times misused in a sterile manner. We know that those who are most vulnerable to environmental degradation are the poor; they are the ones who suffer its most serious consequences. Thus, solidarity means the implementation of effective tools that are able to fight environmental degradation and poverty at the same time. There are many positive experiences in this regard. For example the development and transfer of appropriate technologies that are able to make the best possible use of the human, natural, and socio-economic resources that are most readily available at the local level, in order to ensure their long-term sustainability.

Second, the principle of justice. In *Laudato Si'* I spoke of "ecological debt," especially between the North and South, connected to trade imbalances with consequences in the context of ecology, as well as the disproportionate use of natural resources historically exploited by some countries. We must honor this debt. These nations are called upon to contribute to resolving this debt by setting a good example: by limiting in a significant way the consumption of non-renewable energy; by providing resources to countries in need for the promotion of policies and programs for sustainable development; by adopting appropriate systems for the management of forests, transportation, and waste; by seriously addressing the grave problem of food waste; by favoring a model of a circular economy; and by encouraging new attitudes and lifestyles.

Third, the principle of participation, which requires the involvement of all stakeholders, even of those who often remain at the margins of decision-making. We live, in fact, in a very interesting historical time: on the one hand science and technology place unprecedented power in our hands; on the other, the proper use of this power requires us to adopt a more integral and inclusive vision. This demands that we open the door to dialogue, a dialogue that is inspired by this vision, which is rooted in the integral ecology which is the subject of the encyclical *Laudato Si'*. This is obviously a great cultural, spiritual, and educational challenge. Out of respect for our dignity and for creation: solidarity, justice, and participation.

—*Address to the Environment Ministers of the European Union,*
September 16, 2015

3

Ethical Failure

In our time humanity is experiencing a turning-point in its history, as we can see from the advances being made in so many fields. We can only praise the steps being taken to improve people's welfare in areas such as health care, education, and communications. At the same time we have to remember that the majority of our contemporaries are barely living from day to day, with dire consequences. A number of diseases are spreading. The hearts of many people are gripped by fear and desperation, even in the so-called rich countries. The joy of living frequently fades, lack of respect for others and violence are on the rise, and inequality is increasingly evident. It is a struggle to live and, often, to live with precious little dignity. This epochal change has been set in motion by the enormous qualitative, quantitative, rapid, and cumulative advances occurring in the sciences and in technology, and by their instant application in different areas of nature and of life. We are in an age of knowledge and information, which has led to new and often anonymous kinds of power.

—*Apostolic Exhortation* Evangelii Gaudium, 52, *November 24, 2013*

The Scandal of Hunger

It is a scandal that there is still hunger and malnutrition in the world! It is not just a question of responding to immediate emergencies, but of addressing together, at all levels, a problem that challenges our personal and social conscience, in order to achieve a just and lasting solution. May no one be obliged to abandon his or her country or cultural environment due to a lack of essential means of subsistence! Paradoxically, in an age when globalization enables us to know about the situations of need that exist in the world and to multiply exchanges and human relationships, the tendency to individualism and to withdraw into ourselves seems to be on the rise. These tendencies lead to a certain attitude of indifference—at the personal, institutional, and state level—toward those who are dying of hunger or suffering from malnutrition, almost as though it were an inevitable fact. However, hunger and malnutrition can never be considered a normal occurrence to which one must become accustomed, as if they were part of the system. Something has to change in ourselves, in our mentality, in our societies. What can we do? I think that an important step is to tear down decisively the barriers of individualism, self-withdrawal, and the slavery of profit at all costs; and this needs to be accomplished not only in the dynamics of human relations but also in global economic and financial dynamics. Today more than ever, I think it is necessary *to educate ourselves in solidarity*, to rediscover the value and meaning of this very uncomfortable word, which oftentimes has been left aside, and to make it become a basic attitude in decisions made at the political, economic, and financial levels, in relationships between persons, peoples, and nations. It is only in standing firmly united, by overcoming selfish ways of thinking and partisan interests, that the objective of eliminating forms of indigence determined by a lack of food will also be achieved. [This requires] a solidarity that is not reduced to different forms of welfare, but which makes an effort to ensure that an ever greater number of persons is economically independent. Many steps have been taken in different countries, but we are still far from a world where all can live with dignity...

For this it is indispensable to rethink and renew our food systems from a perspective of solidarity, by overcoming the logic of an unbridled exploitation of creation and by better orienting our commitment to cultivate and care for the environment and its resources, in order to guarantee food security and progress toward sufficient and healthy food for all. This poses a serious question about the need to substantially modify our lifestyle, including the way we eat, which, in so many areas of the planet, is marked by consumerism and the waste and squandering of food. The data provided by FAO [Food and Agriculture Organization of the United Nations] indicates that approximately one third of the global production of food is not available due to increasing loss and wastefulness. Eliminating this waste would drastically reduce the number of people suffering from hunger. Our parents taught us to appreciate what we receive and have and to regard it as a precious gift of God.

However, wasting food is only one of the fruits of the "culture of waste," which often leads to sacrificing men and women to the idols of profit and consumption. It is a sad sign of the "globalization of indifference" that slowly leads us to grow "accustomed" to the suffering of others, as though it were normal. The challenge of hunger and malnutrition does not only have an economic or scientific dimension that has to do with the quantitative and qualitative aspects of the food supply chain; it also and above all has an ethical and anthropological dimension. To educate in solidarity therefore means *to educate ourselves in humanity*. To build a society that is truly human means to put the person and his or her dignity at the center, always, and never to sell him out to the logic of profit. The human being and his dignity are "pillars on which to build shared regulations and structures that, by overcoming pragmatism or the mere technical data, are capable of eliminating divisions and of narrowing existing gaps" (cf. Address to Participants in the 38th Session of the FAO, 20 June 2013).

—*Message for World Food Day, October 16, 2013*

HUNGER FOR DIGNITY

I would like to tell you that the Church, the "advocate of justice and defender of the poor in the face of intolerable social and economic inequalities which cry to heaven" (*Aparecida Document*, 395), wishes to offer her support for every initiative that can signify genuine development for every person and for the whole person. Dear friends, it is certainly necessary to give bread to the hungry—this is an act of justice. But there is also a deeper hunger, the hunger for a happiness that only God can satisfy, the hunger for dignity. There is neither real promotion of the common good nor real human development when there is ignorance of the fundamental pillars that govern a nation, its non-material goods: *life*, which is a gift of God, a value always to be protected and promoted; the *family*, the foundation of coexistence and a remedy against social fragmentation; *integral education*, which cannot be reduced to the mere transmission of information for purposes of generating profit; *health*, which must seek the comprehensive well-being of the person, including the spiritual dimension, which is essential for human balance and healthy coexistence; *security*, in the conviction that violence can be overcome only by changing human hearts.

I would like to add one final point, one final point. Here, as in the whole of Brazil, there are many young people. You young people, my dear young friends, you have a particular sensitivity toward injustice, but you are often disappointed by facts that speak of corruption on the part of people who put their own interests before the common good. To you and to all, I repeat: never yield to discouragement, do not lose trust, do not allow your hope to be extinguished. Situations can change, people can change. Be the first to seek to bring good, do not grow accustomed to evil, but defeat it with good. The Church is with you, bringing you the precious good of faith, bringing Jesus Christ, who "came that they may have life and have it abundantly" (Jn 10:10).

Address to the community of Varginha, Brazil, July 25, 2013

THE IDOLATRY OF PROFITS

It is no longer man who commands, but money, money, cash commands. And God our Father gave us the task of protecting the earth—not for money, but for ourselves: for men and women. We have this task! Nevertheless men and women are sacrificed to the idols of profit and consumption: it is the "culture of waste." If a computer breaks it is a tragedy, but poverty, the needs and dramas of so many people end up being considered normal. If on a winter's night, here on the Via Ottaviano—for example—someone dies, that is not news. If there are children in so many parts of the world who have nothing to eat, that is not news, it seems normal. It cannot be so! And yet these things enter into normality: that some homeless people should freeze to death on the street—this doesn't make news. On the contrary, when the stock market drops ten points in some cities, it constitutes a tragedy. Someone who dies is not news, but lowering income by ten points is a tragedy! In this way people are thrown aside as if they were trash.

This "culture of waste" tends to become a common mentality that infects everyone. Human life, the person, are no longer seen as a primary value to be respected and safeguarded, especially if they are poor or disabled, if they are not yet useful—like the unborn child—or are no longer of any use—like the elderly person. This culture of waste has also made us insensitive to wasting and throwing out excess foodstuffs, which is especially condemnable when, in every part of the world, unfortunately, many people and families suffer hunger and malnutrition. There was a time when our grandparents were very careful not to throw away any leftover food. Consumerism has induced us to be accustomed to excess and to the daily waste of food, whose value, which goes far beyond mere financial parameters, we are no longer able to judge correctly.

Let us remember well, however, that whenever food is thrown out it is as if it were stolen from the table of the poor, from the hungry! I ask everyone to reflect on the problem of the loss and waste of food, to identify ways and approaches which, by seriously dealing with this problem, convey solidarity and sharing with the underprivileged.

—*General Audience, June 5, 2013*

A Culture of Encounter

In my Message for the World Day of Peace (December 8, 2013), dedicated to *fraternity* as the *foundation and pathway to peace*, I observed that "fraternity is generally first learned within the family...," for the family "by its vocation...is meant to spread its love to the world around it," and to contribute to the growth of that spirit of service and sharing which builds peace. This is the message of the crib, where we see the Holy Family, not alone and isolated from the world, but surrounded by shepherds and the Magi, that is, by an open community in which there is room for everyone, poor and rich alike, those near and those afar. In this way we can appreciate the insistence of my beloved predecessor Benedict XVI that "the language of the family is a language of peace" (*Message for World Day of Peace, December 8, 2007*).

Sadly, this is often not the case, as the number of broken and troubled families is on the rise, not simply because of the weakening sense of belonging so typical of today's world, but also because of the adverse conditions in which many families are forced to live, even to the point where they lack basic means of subsistence. There is a need for suitable policies aimed at supporting, assisting, and strengthening the family!

It also happens that the elderly are looked upon as a burden, while young people lack clear prospects for their

lives. Yet the elderly and the young are the hope of humanity. The elderly bring with them wisdom born of experience; the young open us to the future and prevent us from
becoming self-absorbed. It is prudent to keep the elderly
from being ostracized from the life of society, so as to preserve the living memory of all peoples. It is likewise important to invest in the young through suitable initiatives
which can help them to find employment and establish
homes. We must not stifle their enthusiasm! I vividly recall
my experience at the twenty-eighth World Youth Day in Rio
de Janeiro. I met so many happy young people! What great
hope and expectation is present in their eyes and in their
prayers! What a great thirst for life and a desire for openness to others!

Being closed and isolated always makes for a stifling,
heavy atmosphere which sooner or later ends up creating
sadness and oppression. What is needed instead is a shared
commitment to favoring a culture of encounter, for only
those able to reach out to others are capable of bearing fruit,
creating bonds of communion, radiating joy, and being
peacemakers...

Peace is also threatened by every denial of human dignity, first by the lack of access to adequate nutrition. We
cannot be indifferent to those suffering from hunger, especially children, when we think of how much food is wasted
every day in many parts of the world immersed in what I
have often termed "the throwaway culture." Unfortunately,
what is thrown away is not only food and dispensable ob-

jects, but often human beings themselves, who are discarded as "unnecessary."

—Address to the Diplomatic Corps, January 13, 2014

UNACCEPTABLE WASTE

The majority of the men and women of our time still continue to experience daily insecurity, often with dramatic
consequences. In the context of your meeting, I wish to em-
phasize the importance that the various political and economic sectors have in promoting an inclusive approach
which takes into consideration the dignity of every human
person and the common good. I am referring to a concern
that ought to shape every political and economic decision,
but which at times seems to be little more than an after-
thought. Those working in these sectors have a precise responsibility toward others, particularly those who are most
frail, weak, and vulnerable.

It is intolerable that thousands of people continue to die
every day from hunger, even though substantial quantities
of food are available and often simply wasted. Likewise, we
cannot but be moved by the many refugees seeking mini-
mally dignified living conditions, who not only fail to find
hospitality, but often, tragically, perish in moving from
place to place. I know that these words are forceful, even
dramatic, but they seek both to affirm and to challenge the
ability of this assembly to make a difference. In fact, those

who have demonstrated their aptitude for being innovative and for improving the lives of many people by their ingenuity and professional expertise can further contribute by putting their skills at the service of those who are still living in dire poverty.

—*Message to the Executive Chairman of the World Economic Forum,*
January 17, 2014

IMBALANCE IN CONSUMPTION

Doomsday predictions can no longer be met with irony or disdain. We may well be leaving to coming generations debris, desolation, and filth. The pace of consumption, waste, and environmental change has so stretched the planet's capacity that our contemporary lifestyle, unsustainable as it is, can only precipitate catastrophes, such as those which even now periodically occur in different areas of the world. The effects of the present imbalance can be reduced only by our decisive action, here and now. We need to reflect on our accountability before those who will have to endure the dire consequences.

Our difficulty in seriously taking up this challenge has much to do with an ethical and cultural decline that has accompanied the deterioration of the environment. Men and women of our postmodern world run the risk of rampant individualism, and many problems of society are connected with today's self-centered culture of instant gratification. We see this in the crisis of family and social ties and the difficulties of recognizing the other. Parents can be prone to impulsive and wasteful consumption, which then affects their children who find it increasingly difficult to acquire a home of their own and build a family. Furthermore, our inability to think seriously about future generations is linked to our inability to broaden the scope of our present interests and to give consideration to those who remain excluded from development. Let us not only keep the poor of the future in mind, but also today's poor, whose life on this earth is brief and who cannot keep on waiting.

—*Encyclical* Laudato Si', *161–62, May 24, 2015*

4

This Economy Kills

An Economy of Exclusion

Just as the commandment "Thou shalt not kill" sets a clear limit in order to safeguard the value of human life, today we also have to say "thou shalt not" to an economy of exclusion and inequality. Such an economy kills. How can it be that it is not a news item when an elderly homeless person dies of exposure, but it is news when the stock market loses two points? This is a case of exclusion. Can we continue to stand by when food is thrown away while people are starving? This is a case of inequality. Today everything comes under the laws of competition and the survival of the fittest, where the powerful feed upon the powerless. As a consequence, masses of people find themselves excluded and marginalized: without work, without possibilities, without any means of escape.

Human beings are themselves considered consumer goods to be used and then discarded. We have created a

36

"throw-away" culture which is now spreading. It is no longer simply about exploitation and oppression, but something new. Exclusion ultimately has to do with what it means to be a part of the society in which we live; those excluded are no longer society's underside or its fringes or its disenfranchised—they are no longer even a part of it. The excluded are not the "exploited" but the outcast, the "leftovers."

In this context, some people continue to defend trickle-down theories which assume that economic growth, encouraged by a free market, will inevitably succeed in bringing about greater justice and inclusiveness in the world. This opinion, which has never been confirmed by the facts, expresses a crude and naïve trust in the goodness of those wielding economic power and in the sacralized workings of the prevailing economic system. Meanwhile, the excluded are still waiting. To sustain a lifestyle which excludes others, or to sustain enthusiasm for that selfish ideal, a globalization of indifference has developed. Almost without being aware of it, we end up being incapable of feeling compassion at the outcry of the poor, weeping for other people's pain, and feeling a need to help them, as though all this were someone else's responsibility and not our own. The culture of prosperity deadens us; we are thrilled if the market offers us something new to purchase. In the meantime all those lives stunted for lack of opportunity seem a mere spectacle; they fail to move us.

—*Apostolic Exhortation* Evangelii Gaudium, *53–54, November 24, 2013*

THE INVISIBLE TYRANNY

Our human family is presently experiencing something of a turning point in its own history, if we consider the advances made in various areas. We can only praise the positive achievements that contribute to the authentic welfare of mankind in fields such as those of health, education and communications. At the same time, we must also acknowledge that the majority of the men and women of our time continue to live daily in situations of insecurity, with dire consequences. Certain pathologies are increasing, with their psychological consequences; fear and desperation grip the hearts of many people, even in the so-called rich countries; the joy of life is diminishing; indecency and violence are on the rise; poverty is becoming more and more evident. People have to struggle to live and, frequently, to live in an undignified way. One cause of this situation, in my opinion, is in our relationship with money, and our acceptance of its power over ourselves and our society. Consequently the financial crisis that we are experiencing makes us forget that its ultimate origin is to be found in a profound human crisis—in the denial of the primacy of human beings! We have created new idols. The worship of the golden calf of old (cf. Ex 32:15–34) has found a new and heartless image in the cult of money and the dictatorship of an economy that is faceless and lacking any truly humane goal.

The worldwide financial and economic crisis seems to highlight the distortions and above all the gravely deficient human perspective that reduces man to one of his needs alone, namely, consumption. Worse yet, human beings themselves are nowadays considered as consumer goods that can be used and thrown away. We have started a throw-away culture. This tendency is seen on the level of individuals and whole societies—and it is being promoted!

In circumstances like these, solidarity, which is the treasure of the poor, is often considered counterproductive, opposed to the logic of finance and the economy. While the income of a minority is increasing exponentially, that of the majority is crumbling. This imbalance results from ideologies that uphold the absolute autonomy of markets and financial speculation, and thus deny the right of control to states, which are themselves charged with providing for the common good. A new, invisible, and at times virtual tyranny is established, one which unilaterally and irremediably imposes its own laws and rules. Moreover, indebtedness and credit distance countries from their real economy and citizens from their real buying power. Added to this, as if it were needed, is widespread corruption and selfish fiscal evasion which have taken on worldwide dimensions. The will to power and possession has become limitless.

Concealed behind this attitude is a rejection of ethics, a rejection of God. Ethics, like solidarity, is a nuisance! It is regarded as counterproductive: as something too human, because it relativizes money and power; as a threat, because it rejects manipulation and subjection of people, because ethics leads to God, who is situated outside the categories of the market. God is thought to be unmanageable by these financiers, economists, and politicians. God is unmanageable, even dangerous, because he calls man to his full realization and to independence from any kind of slavery. Ethics—naturally, not the ethics of ideology—makes it possible, in my view, to create a balanced social order that is more humane. In this sense, I encourage the financial experts and the political leaders of your countries to consider the words of Saint John Chrysostom: "Not to share one's goods with the poor is to rob them and to deprive them of life. It is not our goods that we possess, but theirs" (*Homily on Lazarus*, 1:6 – *PG* 48, 992D).

There is a need for financial reform along ethical lines that would produce in its turn an economic reform to benefit everyone. This would nevertheless require a courageous change of attitude on the part of political leaders. I urge them to face this challenge with determination and farsightedness, taking account, naturally, of their particular situations. Money has to serve, not to rule! The pope loves everyone, rich and poor alike, but the pope has the duty, in Christ's name, to remind the rich to help the poor, to respect them, to promote them. The pope appeals for disinterested solidarity and for a return to person-centered ethics in the world of finance and economics.

For her part, the Church always works for the integral development of every person. In this sense, she reiterates that the common good should not be simply an extra, simply a conceptual scheme of inferior quality tacked onto political programs. The Church encourages those in power to be truly at the service of the common good of their peoples. She urges financial leaders to take account of ethics and solidarity. And why should they not turn to God to draw inspiration from his designs? In this way, a new political and economic mindset would arise that would help to transform the absolute dichotomy between the economic and social spheres into a healthy symbiosis.

—*Address to New Ambassadors, May 16, 2013*

THE FETISHISM OF MONEY

The Church renews today her strong appeal for the protection of the dignity and centrality of every person, respecting his fundamental rights, as her social doctrine stresses, rights that she requests be really extended where they are not recognized to millions of men and women on every continent. In a world where there is much talk of rights, how many times human dignity is trampled. In a world where there is so much talk of rights, it seems the only one that has them is money. Dear brothers and sisters, we live in a world where money commands. We live in a world, in a culture, where the fetishism of money reigns.

—*Address to the Pontifical Council for the Pastoral Care of Migrants and Travelers, May 24, 2013*

THE DISTORTION OF THE MARKETPLACE

The technocratic paradigm also tends to dominate economic and political life. The economy accepts every advance in technology with a view to profit, without concern for its potentially negative impact on human beings. Finance overwhelms the real economy. The lessons of the global financial crisis have not been assimilated, and we are learning all too slowly the lessons of environmental deterioration. Some circles maintain that current economics and technology will solve all environmental problems, and argue, in popular and non-technical terms, that the problems of global hunger and poverty will be resolved simply by market growth. They are less concerned with certain economic theories that today scarcely anybody dares defend than with their actual operation in the functioning of the economy...

A consumerist vision of human beings, encouraged by the mechanisms of today's globalized economy, has a leveling effect on cultures, diminishing the immense variety which is the heritage of all humanity. Attempts to resolve all problems through uniform regulations or technical interventions can lead to overlooking the complexities of local problems which demand the active participation of all members of the community. New processes taking shape cannot always fit into frameworks imported from outside; they need to be based in the local culture itself. As life and the world are dynamic realities, so our care for the world must also be flexible and dynamic.

Merely technical solutions run the risk of addressing symptoms and not the more serious underlying problems. There is a need to respect the rights of peoples and cultures, and to appreciate that the development of a social group presupposes a historical process which takes place within a cultural context and demands the constant and active involvement of local people *from within their proper culture*. Nor can the notion of the quality of life be imposed from without, for quality of life must be understood within the world of symbols and customs proper to each human group.

—*Encyclical* Laudato Si', *109, 144, May 24, 2015*

ENSURING ECONOMIC FREEDOM

In order to continue providing employment, it is imperative to promote an economy which favors productive diversity and business creativity. For example, there is a great variety of small-scale food production systems which feed the greater part of the world's peoples, using a modest amount of land and producing less waste, be it in small agricultural parcels, in orchards and gardens, hunting and wild harvesting, or local fishing. Economies of scale, especially in the agricultural sector, end up forcing small [scale] holders to sell their land or to abandon their traditional crops. Their attempts to move to other, more diversified, means of production prove fruitless because of the difficulty of linkage with regional and global markets, or because the infrastructure for sales and transport is geared to larger businesses. Civil authorities have the right and duty to adopt clear and firm measures in support of small producers and differentiated production. To ensure economic freedom from which all can effectively benefit, restraints occasionally have to be imposed on those possessing greater resources and financial power. To claim economic freedom while real conditions bar many people from actual access to it, and while possibilities for employment continue to shrink, is to practice a doublespeak which brings politics into disrepute. Business is a noble vocation, directed to producing wealth and improving our world. It can be a fruitful source of prosperity for the areas in which it operates, especially if it sees the creation of jobs as an essential part of its service to the common good.

—*Encyclical* Laudato Si', *109, 129, May 24, 2015*

MONEY MUST SERVE, NOT RULE

The goal of economics and politics is to serve humanity, beginning with the poorest and most vulnerable wherever they may be, even in their mothers' wombs. Every economic and political theory or action must set about providing each inhabitant of the planet with the minimum wherewithal to live in dignity and freedom, with the possibility of supporting a family, educating children, praising God, and developing one's own human potential. This is the main thing; in the absence of such a vision, all economic activity is meaningless.

In this sense, the various grave economic and political challenges facing today's world require a courageous change of attitude that will restore to the end (the human person) and to the means (economics and politics) their proper place. Money and other political and economic means must serve, not rule, bearing in mind that, in a seemingly paradoxical way, free and disinterested solidarity is the key to the smooth functioning of the global economy.

—*Letter to David Cameron, Prime Minister of the United Kingdom,*
June 15, 2013

An Economy at the Service of the People

Human beings and nature must not be at the service of money. Let us say NO to an economy of exclusion and inequality, where money rules, rather than service. That economy kills. That economy excludes. That economy destroys Mother Earth.

The economy should not be a mechanism for accumulating goods, but rather the proper administration of our common home. This entails a commitment to care for that home and to the fitting distribution of its goods among all. It is not only about ensuring a supply of food or "decent sustenance." Nor, although this is already a great step forward, is it to guarantee the three "L's" of land, lodging, and labor for which you are working. A truly communitarian economy, one might say an economy of Christian inspiration, must ensure peoples' dignity and their "general, temporal welfare and prosperity" (Pope John XXIII, *Mater et Magistra*, 3). Pope John XXIII spoke this last phrase fifty years ago, and Jesus says in the gospel that whoever freely offers a glass of water to one who is thirsty will be remembered in the Kingdom of Heaven...

A just economy must create the conditions for everyone to be able to enjoy a childhood without want, to develop their talents when young, to work with full rights during their active years, and to enjoy a dignified retirement as they grow older. It is an economy where human beings, in harmony with nature, structure the entire system of production and distribution in such a way that the abilities and needs of each individual find suitable expression in social life. You, and other peoples as well, sum up this desire in a simple and beautiful expression: "to live well," (*buen vivir*), which is not the same as "to have a good time."

Such an economy is not only desirable and necessary, but also possible. It is no utopia or chimera. It is an extremely realistic prospect. We can achieve it. The available resources in our world, the fruit of the intergenerational labors of peoples and the gifts of creation, more than suffice for the integral development of "each man and the whole man" (Pope Paul VI, *Populorum progressio*, 14.)

The problem is of another kind. There exists a system with different aims, a system which, in addition to irresponsibly accelerating the pace of production, and using industrial and agricultural methods which damage Mother Earth in the name of "productivity," continues to deny many millions of our brothers and sisters their most elementary economic, social, and cultural rights. This system runs counter to the plan of Jesus, against the good news that Jesus brought.

Working for a just distribution of the fruits of the earth and human labor is not mere philanthropy. It is a moral obligation. For Christians, the responsibility is even greater: it is a commandment. It is about giving to the poor and to people what is theirs by right. The universal destination of goods is not a figure of speech found in the Church's social teaching. It is a reality prior to private property. Property, especially when it affects natural resources, must always serve the needs of people. And those needs are not restricted to consumption. It is not enough to let a few drops fall whenever the poor shake a cup which never runs over by itself. Welfare programs geared to certain emergencies can only be considered temporary and incidental responses. They could never replace true inclusion, an inclusion which provides worthy, free, creative, participatory and solidary work.

Along this path, popular movements play an essential role, not only by making demands and lodging protests but even more basically by being creative. You are social poets: creators of work, builders of housing, producers of food, above all for people left behind by the world market.

—Address to the Second World Meeting of Popular Movements,
Santa Cruz de la Sierra, Bolivia, July 9, 2015

AN HONEST ECONOMY

The Church is well aware of the value of cooperatives. At the origin of many of them were priests, committed lay faithful, and communities imbued with the spirit of Christian solidarity. This "movement" has never been exhausted. In the social teaching of the Church there are frequent references to cooperatives. In the encyclical *Laudato Si'* too, I stressed their value in the field of renewable energy and in agriculture (cf. 179–180).

I would like to speak about some points of encouragement, which I addressed to the whole Confederation in February. I will recall them briefly.

First: Continue to be an engine that develops the weakest part of the local communities and of civil society, especially keeping in mind the unemployed young people and aiming to set up new cooperative enterprises.

Second: Take the lead in proposing and in carrying out new welfare solutions, beginning with the field of health care.

Third: Pay attention to the relationship between the economy and social justice, keeping at the center the dignity and value of the person. The person must always be at the center, not the god of money.

Fourth: Facilitate and encourage family life, and propose cooperative and mutual solutions for the management of common goods, which cannot become the property of a few or the object of speculation.

Fifth: Promote the use of money for solidarity and for society, in the style of a true cooperative, where capital does not command over men, but men over capital.

Sixth: The result of all this will make the economy of honesty grow—the economy of honesty at a time in which the air of corruption is everywhere. You are asked not only to be honest—this is normal—but to spread and root honesty in the whole environment, and to fight corruption.

Seventh: Finally, play an active role in globalization, in order to globalize solidarity.

—Address to the personnel of the Cooperative Credit Bank of Rome, September 12, 2015

SOLIDARITY

Solidarity is a word that is not always well received. In certain circumstances it has become a dirty word, something one dares not say. However, it is a word that means much more than an occasional gesture of generosity. It means thinking and acting in terms of community. It means that the lives of all take priority over the appropriation of goods by a few. It also means fighting against the structural causes of poverty and inequality; of the lack of work, land, and housing; and of the denial of social and labor rights. It means confronting the destructive effects of the empire of money: forced dislocation, painful emigration, human trafficking, drugs, war, violence and all those realities that many of you suffer and that we are all called upon to transform. Solidarity, understood in its deepest sense, is a way of making history, and this is what the popular movements are doing...

The scandal of poverty cannot be addressed by promoting strategies of containment that only tranquilize the poor and render them tame and inoffensive. How sad it is when we find, behind allegedly altruistic works, the other being reduced to passivity or being negated; or worse still, we find hidden personal agendas or commercial interests. "Hypocrites" is what Jesus would say to those responsible. How marvelous it is, by contrast, when we see peoples moving forward, especially their young and their poorest members. Then one feels a promising breeze that revives hope for a better world. May this breeze become a cyclone of hope. This is my wish.

—*Address to the World Meeting of Popular Movements,*
Rome, October 28, 2014

Inequality, the Root of Social Ills

The need to resolve the structural causes of poverty cannot be delayed, not only for the pragmatic reason of its urgency for the good order of society but because society needs to be cured of a sickness which is weakening and frustrating it, and which can only lead to new crises. Welfare projects, which meet certain urgent needs, should be considered merely temporary responses. As long as the problems of the poor are not radically resolved by rejecting the absolute autonomy of markets and financial speculation and by attacking the structural causes of inequality, no solution will be found for the world's problems or, for that matter, for any problems. Inequality is the root of social ills.

The dignity of each human person and the pursuit of the common good are concerns which ought to shape all economic policies. At times, however, they seem to be a mere addendum imported from without in order to fill out a political discourse lacking in perspectives or plans for true and integral development. How many words prove irksome to this system! It is irksome when the question of ethics is raised, when global solidarity is invoked, when the distribution of goods is mentioned, when reference is made to protecting labor and defending the dignity of the powerless, when allusion is made to a God who demands a commitment to justice. At other times these issues are exploited by a rhetoric which cheapens them. Casual indifference in the face of such questions empties our lives and our words of all meaning. Business is a vocation, and a noble vocation, provided that those engaged in it see themselves challenged by a greater meaning in life; this will enable them truly to serve the common good by striving to increase the goods of this world and to make them more accessible to all.

We can no longer trust in the unseen forces and the invisible hand of the market. Growth in justice requires more than economic growth, while presupposing such growth. It requires decisions, programs, mechanisms, and processes specifically geared to a better distribution of income, the creation of sources of employment, and an integral promotion of the poor which goes beyond a simple welfare mentality. I am far from proposing an irresponsible populism, but the economy can no longer turn to remedies that are a new poison, such as attempting to increase profits by reducing the work force and thereby adding to the ranks of the excluded.

If anyone feels offended by my words, I would respond that I speak them with affection and with the best of intentions, quite apart from any personal interest or political ideology. My words are not those of a foe or an opponent. I am interested only in helping those who are in thrall to an individualistic, indifferent, and self-centered mentality to be freed from those unworthy chains and to attain a way of living and thinking which is more humane, noble and fruitful, and which will bring dignity to their presence on this earth.

—*Apostolic Exhortation* Evangelii Gaudium, *202, 203, 204, 208,*
November 24, 2013

5

The Globalization of Indifference

INSENSIBILITY TO THE SUFFERING OF THE OTHER

"Where is your brother?" Who is responsible for this blood? In Spanish literature we have a comedy of Lope de Vega which tells how the people of the town of Fuente Ovejuna kill their governor because he is a tyrant. They do it in such a way that no one knows who the actual killer is. So when the royal judge asks, "Who killed the governor?" they all reply, "Fuente Ovejuna, sir." Everybody and nobody!

Today too, the question has to be asked: Who is responsible for the blood of these brothers and sisters of ours? Nobody! That is our answer: It isn't me; I don't have anything to do with it; it must be someone else, but certainly not me. Yet God is asking each of us: "Where is the blood of your brother which cries out to me?"

Today no one in our world feels responsible; we have lost a sense of responsibility for our brothers and sisters. We have fallen into the hypocrisy of the priest and the

53

Levite whom Jesus described in the parable of the Good Samaritan: we see our brother half dead on the side of the road, and perhaps we say to ourselves: "Poor soul...!", and then go on our way. It's not our responsibility, and with that we feel reassured, assuaged. The culture of comfort, which makes us think only of ourselves, makes us insensitive to the cries of other people, makes us live in soap bubbles which, however lovely, are insubstantial... offers a fleeting and empty illusion which results in indifference to others. Indeed, it even leads to the globalization of indifference. In this globalized world, we have fallen into globalized indifference. We have become used to the suffering of others: it doesn't affect me; it doesn't concern me; it's none of my business!

—Homily at the Island of Lambedusa
(a point of entry for immigrants, many of whom drown at sea), July 8, 2013

THE WORLD OF THE EXCLUDED

Today we are living in a world which is growing ever "smaller" and where, as a result, it would seem to be easier for all of us to be neighbors. Developments in travel and communications technology are bringing us closer together and making us more connected, even as globalization makes us increasingly interdependent. Nonetheless, divisions, which are sometimes quite deep, continue to exist within our human family. On the global level we see a scandalous gap between the opulence of the wealthy and the utter destitution of the poor. Often we need only walk the streets of a city to see the contrast between people living on the street and the brilliant lights of the store windows. We have become so accustomed to these things that they no longer unsettle us. Our world suffers from many forms of exclusion, marginalization, and poverty, to say nothing of conflicts born of a combination of economic, political, ideological, and, sadly, even religious motives.

—*Message for World Communications Day, January 24, 2014*

Abandoned to the Laws of Economy

Among our tasks as witnesses to the love of Christ is that of giving a voice to the cry of the poor, so that they are not abandoned to the laws of an economy that seems at times to treat people as mere consumers.

—*Address to His Grace Justin Welby, Archbishop of Canterbury, June 14, 2013*

The Cry of the Poor

Our faith in Christ, who became poor and was always close to the poor and the outcast, is the basis of our concern for the integral development of society's most neglected members.

Each individual Christian and every community is called to be an instrument of God for the liberation and promotion of the poor, and for enabling them to be fully a part of society. This demands that we be docile and attentive to the cry of the poor and come to their aid. A mere glance at the scriptures is enough to make us see how our gracious Father wants to hear the cry of the poor: "I have observed the misery of my people who are in Egypt; I have heard their cry on account of their taskmasters. Indeed, I know their sufferings, and I have come down to deliver them...so I will send you..." (Ex 3:7–8, 10). We also see how he is concerned for their needs: "When the Israelites cried out to the Lord, the Lord raised up for them a deliverer" (Jg 3:15). If we, who are God's means of hearing the poor, turn deaf ears to this plea, we oppose the Father's will and his plan; that poor person "might cry to the Lord against you, and you would incur guilt" (Dt 15:9). A lack of solidarity toward his or her needs will directly affect our relationship with God: "For if in bitterness of soul he calls down a curse upon you, his Creator will hear his prayer" (Sir 4:6). The old question always returns: "How does God's love abide in anyone who has the world's goods, and sees a brother or sister in need and yet refuses help?" (1 Jn 3:17). Let us recall also how bluntly the apostle James speaks of the cry of the oppressed: "The wages of the laborers who mowed your fields, which you kept back by fraud, cry out, and the cries of the harvesters have reached the ears of the Lord of hosts" (5:4).

The Church has realized that the need to heed this plea is itself born of the liberating action of grace within each of us, and thus it is not a question of a mission reserved only to a few: "The Church, guided by the gospel of mercy and by love for mankind, hears the cry for justice and intends to respond to it with all her might" (*Libertatis nuntias*, 6). In this context we can understand Jesus' command to his disciples: "You yourselves give them something to eat!" (Mk 6:37): it means working to eliminate the structural causes of poverty and to promote the integral development of the poor, as well as small daily acts of solidarity in meeting the real needs which we encounter. The word "solidarity" is a little worn and at times poorly understood, but it refers to something more than a few sporadic acts of generosity. It presumes the creation of a new mindset that thinks in terms of community and the priority of the life of all over the appropriation of goods by a few.

—*Apostolic Exhortation* Evangelii Gaudium, *186–88, November 24, 2013*

THE CRY OF THE EARTH

These situations have caused Sister Earth, along with all the abandoned of our world, to cry out, pleading that we take another course. Never have we so hurt and mistreated our common home as we have in the last two hundred years. Yet we are called to be instruments of God our Father, so that our planet might be what he desired when he created it and correspond with his plan for peace, beauty, and fullness. The problem is that we still lack the culture needed to confront this crisis. We lack leadership capable of striking out on new paths and meeting the needs of the present with concern for all and without prejudice toward coming generations. The establishment of a legal framework which can set clear boundaries and ensure the protection of ecosystems has become indispensable; otherwise, the new power structures based on the techno-economic paradigm may overwhelm not only our politics but also freedom and justice.

—*Encyclical* Laudato Si', *53, May 24, 2015*

THE SPREAD OF INEQUALITY

The created things of this world are not free of ownership: "For they are yours, O Lord, who love the living" (Wis 11:26). This is the basis of our conviction that, as part of the universe, called into being by one Father, all of us are linked by unseen bonds and together form a kind of universal family, a sublime communion which fills us with a sacred, affectionate, and humble respect . . .

This is not to put all living beings on the same level nor to deprive human beings of their unique worth and the tremendous responsibility it entails. Nor does it imply a divinization of the earth which would prevent us from working on it and protecting it in its fragility. Such notions would end up creating new imbalances that would deflect us from the reality which challenges us.

At times we see an obsession with denying any preeminence to the human person; more zeal is shown in protecting other species than in defending the dignity which all human beings share in equal measure. Certainly, we should be concerned lest other living beings be treated irresponsibly. But we should be particularly indignant at the enormous inequalities in our midst, whereby we continue to tolerate some considering themselves more worthy than others. We fail to see that some are mired in desperate and degrading poverty, with no way out, while others have not the faintest idea of what to do with their possessions, vainly showing off their supposed superiority and leaving behind them so much waste which, if it were the case everywhere, would destroy the planet. In practice, we continue to tolerate that some consider themselves more human than others, as if they had been born with greater rights.

—*Encyclical* Laudato Si', *88–90, May 24, 2015*

CULTIVATING JUSTICE

Nowadays there is much talk of rights, frequently neglecting duties; perhaps we have paid too little heed to those who are hungry. It is also painful to see that the fight against hunger and malnutrition is hindered by "market priorities," the "primacy of profit," which have reduced foodstuffs to a commodity like any other, subject to speculation, also of a financial nature. And while we speak of new rights, the hungry are waiting at the street corner, asking for the right to citizenship, asking for due consideration of their status, to receive a healthy, basic diet. They ask for dignity, not for alms.

These criteria cannot remain in the limbo of theory. Individuals and peoples ask that justice be put into practice: not only in the legal sense, but also in terms of contribution and distribution. Therefore, development plans and the work of international organizations must take into consideration the wish, so frequent among ordinary people, for respect for fundamental human rights in all circumstances and, in this case, the rights of the hungry person. When this is achieved, then humanitarian intervention, emergency relief and development operations—in their truest, fullest sense—will attain greater momentum and yield the desired results.

Interest in the production, availability, and accessibility of foodstuffs, in climate change and in agricultural trade should certainly inspire rules and technical measures, but the first concern must be the individual person who lacks daily nourishment, who has given up thinking about life, family, and social relationships, and instead fights only for survival. At the inauguration of the First Conference on Nutrition in this hall in 1992, St. Pope John Paul II warned the international community of the risk of the "paradox of abundance," in which there is food for everyone, but not everyone can eat, while waste, excessive consumption, and the use of food for other purposes is visible before our very eyes. This is the paradox! Unfortunately, this "paradox" persists. There are few subjects about which there are as many fallacies as there are about hunger, few topics as likely to be manipulated by data, by statistics, by national security demands, by corruption, or by grim references to the economic crisis.

— *Address to the Food and Agriculture Organization of the United Nations, Rome, November 20, 2014*

THE TEMPTATION OF A FALSE PEACE

Peace in society cannot be understood as pacification or the mere absence of violence resulting from the domination of one part of society over others. Nor does true peace act as a pretext for justifying a social structure which silences or appeases the poor, so that the more affluent can placidly support their lifestyle while others have to make do as they can. Demands involving the distribution of wealth, concern for the poor, and human rights cannot be suppressed under the guise of creating a consensus on paper or a transient peace for a contented minority. The dignity of the human person and the common good rank higher than the comfort of those who refuse to renounce their privileges. When these values are threatened, a prophetic voice must be raised.

— *Apostolic Exhortation* Evangelii Gaudium, *218, November 24, 2013*

6

Redefining Progress

We Need a Change

Before all else, let us begin by acknowledging that change is needed. Here I would clarify, lest there be any misunderstanding, that I am speaking about problems common to all Latin Americans and, more generally, to humanity as a whole. They are global problems which today no one state can resolve on its own. With this clarification, I now propose that we ask the following questions:

Do we truly realize that something is wrong in a world where there are so many farmworkers without land, so many families without a home, so many laborers without rights, so many persons whose dignity is not respected?

Do we realize that something is wrong where so many senseless wars are being fought and acts of fratricidal violence are taking place on our very doorstep? Do we realize something is wrong when the soil, water, air and living creatures of our world are under constant threat?

So, if we do realize all this, let's not be afraid to say it: we need change; we want change...

We want change in our lives, in our neighborhoods, in our everyday reality. We want a change that can affect the entire world, since global interdependence calls for global answers to local problems. The globalization of hope, a hope which springs up from peoples and takes root among the poor, must replace the globalization of exclusion and indifference!

Today I wish to reflect with you on the change we want and need. You know that recently I wrote about the problems of climate change. But now I would like to speak of change in another sense. Positive change, a change which is good for us, a change—we can say—which is redemptive. Because we need it. I know that you are looking for change, and not just you alone: in my different meetings, in my different travels, I have sensed an expectation, a longing, a yearning for change in people throughout the world. Even within that ever smaller minority which believes that the present system is beneficial, there is a widespread sense of dissatisfaction and even despondency. Many people are hoping for a change capable of releasing them from the bondage of individualism and the despondency it spawns.

—*Address to the Second World Meeting of Popular Movements, Santa Cruz de la Sierra, Bolivia, July 9, 2015*

PROCESS OF CHANGE

Here in Bolivia I have heard a phrase that I like: "process of change." Change seen not as something which will one day result from any one political decision or change in social structure. We know from painful experience that changes of structure that are not accompanied by a sincere conversion of mind and heart sooner or later end up in bureaucratization, corruption, and failure. There must be a change of heart. That is why I like the image of a "process," processes, where the drive to sow, to water seeds that others will see sprout, replaces the ambition to occupy every available position of power and to see immediate results. The option is to bring about processes and not to occupy positions. Each of us is just one part of a complex and differentiated whole, interacting in time: peoples who struggle to find meaning, a destiny, and to live with dignity, to "live well," and in that sense, worthily.

As members of popular movements, you carry out your work inspired by fraternal love, which you show in opposing social injustice. When we look into the eyes of the suffering, when we see the faces of the endangered campesino, the poor laborer, the downtrodden native, the homeless family, the persecuted migrant, the unemployed young person, the exploited child, the mother who lost her child in a shootout because the barrio was occupied by drug-dealers, the father who lost his daughter to enslavement... when we think of all those names and faces, our hearts break because of so much sorrow and pain. And we are deeply moved, all of us...We are moved because "we have seen and heard" not a cold statistic but the pain of a suffering humanity, our own pain, our own flesh. This is something quite different from abstract theorizing or eloquent indignation. It moves us; it makes us attentive to others in an effort to move forward together. That emotion which turns into community action is not something that can be understood by reason alone: it has a surplus of meaning which only peoples understand, and it gives a special feel to genuine popular movements.

—*Address to the Second World Meeting of Popular Movements,*
Santa Cruz de la Sierra, Bolivia, July 9, 2015

For a Better World

What is involved in the creation of "a better world"? The expression does not allude naively to abstract notions or unattainable ideals; rather, it aims at an authentic and integral development, at efforts to provide dignified living conditions for everyone, at finding just responses to the needs of individuals and families, and at ensuring that God's gift of creation is respected, safeguarded, and cultivated...

Our hearts do desire something "more." Beyond greater knowledge or possessions, they want to "be" more. Development cannot be reduced to economic growth alone, often attained without a thought for the poor and the vulnerable. A better world will come about only if attention is first paid to individuals; if human promotion is integral, taking account of every dimension of the person, including the spiritual; if no one is neglected, including the poor, the sick, prisoners, the needy, and the stranger (cf. Mt 25:31–46); if we can prove capable of leaving behind a throwaway culture and embracing one of encounter and acceptance...

While encouraging the development of a better world, we cannot remain silent about the scandal of poverty in its various forms. Violence, exploitation, discrimination, marginalization, restrictive approaches to fundamental freedoms, whether of individuals or of groups: these are some of the chief elements of poverty which need to be overcome. Often these are precisely the elements which mark migratory movements, thus linking migration to poverty. Fleeing from situations of extreme poverty or persecution in the hope of a better future, or simply to save their own lives, millions of persons choose to migrate. Despite their hopes and expectations, they often encounter mistrust, rejection, and exclusion, to say nothing of tragedies and disasters which offend their human dignity.

—*Message for the World Day of Migrants and Refugees, August 5, 2013*

LOOKING FOR PROGRESS IN A NEW WAY

Ecological culture cannot be reduced to a series of urgent and partial responses to the immediate problems of pollution, environmental decay, and the depletion of natural resources. There needs to be a distinctive way of looking at things, a way of thinking, policies, an educational program, a lifestyle, and a spirituality which together generate resistance to the assault of the technocratic paradigm. Otherwise, even the best ecological initiatives can find themselves caught up in the same globalized logic.

To seek only a technical remedy to each environmental problem which comes up is to separate what is in reality interconnected and to mask the true and deepest problems of the global system...

All of this shows the urgent need for us to move forward in a bold cultural revolution. Science and technology are not neutral; from the beginning to the end of a process, various intentions and possibilities are in play and can take on distinct shapes.

Nobody is suggesting a return to the Stone Age, but we do need to slow down and look at reality in a different way, to appropriate the positive and sustainable progress that has been made, but also to recover the values and the great goals swept away by our unrestrained delusions of grandeur.

—*Encyclical* Laudato Si', *111, 114, May 24, 2015*

INTERACTION BETWEEN THE STATE AND THE PEOPLE

It must be acknowledged that none of the grave problems of humanity can be resolved without interaction between states and peoples at the international level. Every significant action carried out in one part of the planet has universal, ecological, social, and cultural repercussions. Even crime and violence have become globalized. Consequently, no government can act independently of a common responsibility. If we truly desire positive change, we have to humbly accept our interdependence, that is to say, our healthy interdependence. Interaction, however, is not the same as imposition; it is not the subordination of some to serve the interests of others. Colonialism, both old and new, which reduces poor countries to mere providers of raw material and cheap labor, engenders violence, poverty, forced migrations, and all the evils that go hand in hand with these, precisely because, by placing the periphery at the service of the center, it denies those countries the right to an integral development. That is inequality, brothers and sisters, and inequality generates a violence which no police, military, or intelligence resources can control.

Let us say NO, then, to forms of colonialism old and new. Let us say YES to the encounter between peoples and cultures. Blessed are the peacemakers.

—Address to the Second World Meeting of Popular Movements,
Santa Cruz de la Sierra, Bolivia, July 9, 2015

FAR-SIGHTED POLITICS

A healthy politics is sorely needed, capable of reforming and coordinating institutions, promoting best practices, and overcoming undue pressure and bureaucratic inertia. It should be added, though, that even the best mechanisms can break down when there are no worthy goals and values, or a genuine and profound humanism to serve as the basis of a noble and generous society...

What is needed is a politics which is far-sighted and capable of a new, integral, and interdisciplinary approach to handling the different aspects of the crisis. Often, politics itself is responsible for the disrepute in which it is held, on account of corruption and the failure to enact sound public policies. If in a given region the state does not carry out its responsibilities, some business groups can come forward in the guise of benefactors, wield real power, and consider themselves exempt from certain rules, to the point of tolerating different forms of organized crime, human trafficking, the drug trade, and violence, all of which become very difficult to eradicate. If politics shows itself incapable of breaking such a perverse logic and remains caught up in inconsequential discussions, we will continue to avoid facing the major problems of humanity. A strategy for real change calls for rethinking processes in their entirety, for it is not enough to include a few superficial ecological considerations while failing to question the logic that underlies present-day culture. A healthy politics needs to be able to take up this challenge.

—*Encyclical* Laudato Si', *181, 197, May 24, 2015*

7

The Search for the Common Good

THE PRINCIPLE OF THE COMMON GOOD

Each of us here shares a calling to work for the common good. Fifty years ago, the Second Vatican Council defined the common good as "the sum of those conditions of social life which allow social groups and their individual members relatively thorough and ready access to their own fulfillment." I thank you for striving—in your work and your mission—to enable individuals and society to develop and find fulfillment. I am certain that you seek what is beautiful, true, and good in your service of the common good. May your efforts contribute to the growth of greater respect for the human person, endowed with basic and inalienable rights ordered to his or her integral development, and social peace, namely, the stability and security provided by a certain order which cannot be achieved without particular concern for distributive justice (cf. *Laudato Si'*, 157). In a word, let wealth be shared.

—*Meeting with civil authorities, La Paz, Bolivia, July 8, 2015*

WELFARE AND THE COMMON GOOD

We need to be on the alert because it is very easy for us to become accustomed to the atmosphere of inequality all around us, with the result that we take it for granted. Without even being conscious of it, we confuse the "common good" with "prosperity," and so it goes, sliding bit by bit, and the ideal of the "common good" gets lost, ending up in "prosperity," especially when we are the ones who enjoy that prosperity, and not the others. Prosperity understood only in terms of material wealth has a tendency to become selfish; it tends to defend private interests, to be unconcerned about others, and to give free rein to consumerism. Understood in this way, prosperity, instead of helping, breeds conflict and social disintegration; as it becomes more prevalent, it opens the door to the evil of corruption, which brings so much discouragement and damage in its wake. The common good, on the other hand, is much more than the sum of individual interests. It moves from "what is best for me" to "what is best for everyone." It embraces everything that brings a people together: common purpose, shared values, ideas that help us to look beyond our limited individual horizons.

Different social groups have a responsibility to work for unity and the development of society. Freedom is always the best environment for thinkers, civic associations, and the communications media to carry out their activities with passion and creativity in service of the common good. Christians too, are called to be a leaven within society, to bring it their message. The light of Christ's gospel is not the property of the Church; the Church is at the service of the gospel: she must serve the gospel of Christ, so that it can reach the ends of the earth. Faith is a light which does not blind; ideologies blind, faith does not blind; it is a light which does not confuse, but which illuminates and respectfully guides the consciences and history of every person and society... Religious freedom—a phrase we often encounter in civil discourse—also reminds us that faith cannot be restricted to a purely subjective experience. It is not a subculture. The challenge for us will be to help foster the growth of spirituality and commitment of the faith, of Christian commitment in social projects, in deepening the common good, through social projects...

A nation that seeks the common good cannot be closed in on itself; societies are strengthened by networks of relationships. The current problem of immigration makes this clear. These days it is essential to improve diplomatic relations between the countries of the region, in order to avoid conflicts between sister peoples and to advance frank and open dialogue about their problems...Dialogue is essential. Instead of raising walls, we need to be building bridges. Building bridges instead of raising walls. All these issues, thorny as they may be, can find shared solutions; solutions which are reasonable, equitable, and lasting. And in any event, they should never be a cause for aggression, resentment, or enmity; these only worsen situations and stand in the way of their resolution.

—*Meeting with civil authorities, La Paz, Bolivia, July 8, 2015*

BUILDING BRIDGES

As you know, there are various reasons why I chose the name of Francis of Assisi, a familiar figure far beyond the borders of Italy and Europe, even among those who do not profess the Catholic faith. One of the first reasons was Francis's love for the poor. How many poor people there still are in the world! And what great suffering they have to endure! After the example of Francis of Assisi, the Church in every corner of the globe has always tried to care for and look after those who suffer from want, and I think that in many of your countries you can attest to the generous activity of Christians who dedicate themselves to helping the sick, orphans, the homeless, and all the marginalized, thus striving to make society more humane and more just.

But there is another form of poverty! It is the spiritual poverty of our time, which afflicts the so-called richer countries particularly seriously. It is what my much-loved predecessor, Benedict XVI, called the "tyranny of relativism," which makes everyone his own criterion and endangers the coexistence of peoples. And that brings me to a second reason for my name.

Francis of Assisi tells us we should work to build peace. But there is no true peace without truth! There cannot be true peace if everyone is his own criterion, if everyone can always claim exclusively his own rights, without at the same time caring for the good of others, of everyone, on the basis of the nature that unites every human being on this earth.

One of the titles of the bishop of Rome is "pontiff," that is, a builder of bridges with God and between people. My wish is that the dialogue between us should help to build bridges connecting all people, in such a way that everyone can see in the other not an enemy, not a rival, but a brother or sister to be welcomed and embraced!

My own origins impel me to work for the building of bridges. As you know, my family is of Italian origin; and so this dialogue between places and cultures a great distance apart matters greatly to me, this dialogue between one end of the world and the other, which today are growing ever closer, more interdependent, more in need of opportunities to meet and to create real spaces of authentic fraternity.

In this work, the role of religion is fundamental. It is not possible to build bridges between people while forgetting God. But the converse is also true: it is not possible to establish true links with God while ignoring other people. Hence it is important to intensify dialogue among the various religions...And it is also important to intensify outreach to non-believers, so that the differences which divide and hurt us may never prevail, but rather the desire to build true links of friendship between all peoples, despite their diversity.

—*Address to the Diplomatic Corps, March 22, 2013*

THE EARTH AND THE COMMON GOOD

The common good also includes the earth, a central theme of the encyclical which I recently wrote in order to "enter into dialogue with all people about our common home" (*Laudato Si'*, 3). "We need a conversation which includes everyone, since the environmental challenge we are undergoing, and its human roots, concern and affect us all" (ibid., 14).

In *Laudato Si'*, I call for a courageous and responsible effort to "redirect our steps" (ibid., 61) and to avert the most serious effects of the environmental deterioration caused by human activity...Now is the time for courageous actions and strategies aimed at implementing a "culture of care" (ibid., 231) and "an integrated approach to combating poverty, restoring dignity to the excluded, and at the same time protecting nature" (ibid., 139). "We have the freedom needed to limit and direct technology" (ibid., 112), "to devise intelligent ways of...developing and limiting our power" (ibid., 78), and to put technology "at the service of another type of progress, one which is healthier, more human, more social, more integral" (ibid., 112).

—*Address to the U.S. Congress, Washington, DC, September 24, 2015*

WORKING FOR THE RIGHTS OF ALL

Promoting the dignity of the person means recognizing that he or she possesses inalienable rights which no one may take away arbitrarily, much less for the sake of economic interests.

At the same time, however, care must be taken not to fall into certain errors which can arise from a misunderstanding of the concept of human rights and from its misuse. Today there is a tendency to claim ever broader individual rights—I am tempted to say individualistic; underlying this is a conception of the human person as detached from all social and anthropological contexts, as if the person were a "monad," increasingly unconcerned with other surrounding "monads." The equally essential and complementary concept of duty no longer seems to be linked to such a concept of rights. As a result, the rights of the individual are upheld, without regard for the fact that each human being is part of a social context wherein his or her rights and duties are bound up with those of others and with the common good of society itself.

I believe, therefore, that it is vital to develop a culture of human rights which wisely links the individual, or better, the personal aspect, to that of the *common good*, of the *"all of us"* made up of individuals, families, and intermediate groups who together constitute society. In fact, unless the rights of each individual are harmoniously ordered to the greater good, those rights will end up being considered limitless and consequently will become a source of conflicts and violence.

—*Address to the European Parliament, November 25, 2014*

Thinking about Future Generations

The notion of the common good also extends to future generations. The global economic crises have made painfully obvious the detrimental effects of disregarding our common destiny, which cannot exclude those who come after us. We can no longer speak of sustainable development apart from intergenerational solidarity. Once we start to think about the kind of world we are leaving to future generations, we look at things differently; we realize that the world is a gift which we have freely received and must share with others. Since the world has been given to us, we can no longer view reality in a purely utilitarian way, in which efficiency and productivity are entirely geared to our individual benefit. Intergenerational solidarity is not optional, but rather a basic question of justice, since the world we have received also belongs to those who will follow us...

What kind of world do we want to leave to those who come after us, to children who are now growing up? This question not only concerns the environment in isolation; the issue cannot be approached piecemeal. When we ask ourselves what kind of world we want to leave behind, we think in the first place of its general direction, its meaning and its values. Unless we struggle with these deeper issues, I do not believe that our concern for ecology will produce significant results. But if these issues are courageously faced, we are led inexorably to ask other pointed questions:

What is the purpose of our life in this world? Why are we here? What is the goal of our work and all our efforts? What need does the earth have of us? It is no longer enough, then, simply to state that we should be concerned for future generations. We need to see that what is at stake is our own dignity. Leaving an inhabitable planet to future generations is, first and foremost, up to us. The issue is one that dramatically affects us, for it has to do with the ultimate meaning of our earthly sojourn.

—*Encyclical* Laudato Si', *15–60, May 24, 2015*

8

Toward a Culture of Integral Ecology

DEFENDING MOTHER EARTH

Our common home is being pillaged, laid waste, and harmed with impunity. Cowardice in defending [this] is a grave sin. We see with growing disappointment how one international summit after another takes place without any significant result. There exists a clear, definite, and pressing ethical imperative to implement what has not yet been done. We cannot allow certain interests—interests which are global but not universal—to take over, to dominate states and international organizations, and to continue destroying creation. People and their movements are called to cry out, to mobilize and to demand—peacefully, but firmly—that appropriate and urgently needed measures be taken. I ask you, in the name of God, to defend Mother Earth. I have duly addressed this issue in my encyclical letter *Laudato Si'* . . .

The future of humanity does not lie solely in the hands of great leaders, great powers, and the elites. It is fundamentally in the hands of peoples and in their ability to organize. It is in their hands, which can guide with humility and conviction this process of change.

—Address to World Meeting of Popular Movements,
Santa Cruz de la Sierra, Bolivia, July 9, 2015

A FAR-REACHING VISION

The natural environment is closely related to the social, political, and economic environment. It is urgent for all of us to lay the foundations of an integral ecology—this is a question of health—an integral ecology capable of respecting all these human dimensions in resolving the grave social and environmental issues of our time. Otherwise, the glaciers of those mountains will continue to recede, and our sense of gratitude and responsibility with regard to these gifts, our concern for the world we want to leave to future generations, for its meaning and values, will melt just like those glaciers (cf. *Laudato Si'*, 159–60). And we need be aware of this. An integral ecology—I am going out on a limb here—supposes an ecology of Mother Earth: taking care of Mother Earth; with a human ecology: taking care of ourselves; and with a social ecology, in the strong sense of the word.

Because everything is related, we need one another. If politics is dominated by financial speculation, or if the economy is ruled solely by a technocratic and utilitarian paradigm concerned with maximum production, we will not grasp, much less resolve, the great problems of humanity. Cultural life has an important role to play in this regard, for it has to do not only with the development of the mind through the sciences and the creation of beauty through the arts, but also esteem for the local traditions of a people—this is also culture—which are so expressive of the milieu in which they arose and emerged, and the milieu which gives them meaning. There is also need for an ethical and moral education that can cultivate solidarity and shared responsibility between individuals. We should acknowledge the specific role of the religions in the development of culture and the benefits which can they can bring to society. We Christians in particular, as disciples of the good news, are bearers of a message of salvation, which has the ability to ennoble and to inspire great ideals. In this way, it leads to ways of acting that transcend individual interest, readiness to make sacrifices for the sake of others, sobriety and other virtues that develop in us the ability to live as one.

—*Meeting with civil authorities, La Paz, Bolivia, July 8, 2015*

ECOLOGICAL EDUCATION

Here, in this university setting, it would be worthwhile reflecting on the way we educate about this earth of ours, which cries out to heaven.

Our academic institutions are seedbeds, places full of possibility, fertile soil to be cared for, cultivated, and protected. Fertile soil thirsting for life.

My question to you, as educators, is this: Do you watch over your students, helping them to develop a critical sense, an open mind capable of caring for today's world? A spirit capable of seeking new answers to the varied challenges that society sets before humanity today? Are you able to encourage them not to disregard the world around them, what is happening all over? Can you encourage them to do that? To make that possible, you need to take them outside the university lecture hall. Their minds need to leave the classroom, their hearts must go out of the classroom. Does our life, with its uncertainties, its mysteries and its questions, find a place in the university curriculum or different academic activities? Do we enable and support a constructive debate that fosters dialogue in the pursuit of a more humane world? Dialogue, that bridge word, that word which builds bridges.

One avenue of reflection involves all of us, family, schools, and teachers. How do we help our young people not to see a university degree as synonymous with higher status, with more money or social prestige? It is not synonymous with that. How can we help make their education a mark of greater responsibility in the face of today's problems, the needs of the poor, concern for the environment?

I also have a question for you, dear students who are here. You are the seedbed of your society's future growth. Do you realize that this time of study is not only a right, but also a privilege which you have? How many of your friends, known or unknown, would like to have a place in this house but, for various reasons, do not? To what extent do our studies help us and bring us to feel solidarity with them? Ask these questions, dear students.

Educational communities play a fundamental role, an essential role in the enrichment of civic and cultural life. Be careful! It is not enough to analyze and describe reality: there is a need to shape environments of creative thinking, discussions that develop alternatives to current problems, especially today. We need to move to the concrete.

Faced with the globalization of a technocratic paradigm which tends to believe that "every increase in power means an increase of progress itself, an advance in security, useful-ness, welfare and vigor;...an assimilation of new values into the stream of culture, as if reality, goodness, and truth automatically flow from technological and economic power as such" (*Laudato Si'*, 105), it is urgent today for you, for me, for everyone, to keep reflecting on and talking about our current situation. And I am saying "urgent" that we be mo-tivated to think about the culture, the kind of culture we want not only for ourselves, but for our children and our grandchildren. We have received this earth as an inheri-tance, as a gift, in trust. We would do well to ask ourselves: "What kind of world do we want to leave behind? What meaning or direction do we want to give to our lives? Why have we been put here? What is the purpose of our work and all our efforts?" (ibid., 160). Why are we studying?

Personal initiatives are always necessary and good. But we are asked to go one step further: to start viewing reality in an organic and not fragmented way, to ask about where we stand in relation to others, inasmuch as "everything is interconnected" (ibid., 138). There is no right to exclusion.

As a university, as educational institutions, as teachers and students, life itself challenges us to answer these two questions: What does this world need us for? Where is your brother?

May the Holy Spirit inspire and accompany us, for he has summoned us, invited us, given us the opportunity and the duty to offer the best of ourselves. He is the same Spirit who on the first day of creation moved over the waters, ready to transform them, ready to bestow life. He is the same Spirit who gave the disciples the power of Pentecost. The Spirit does not abandon us. He becomes one with us, so that we can encounter paths of new life. May he, the Spirit, always be our companion and our teacher along the way.

—Address to the Pontifical Catholic University of Ecuador, Quito,
July 7, 2015

LIFESTYLES FOR CHANGING THE WORLD

A change in lifestyle could bring healthy pressure to bear on those who wield political, economic, and social power. This is what consumer movements accomplish by boycotting certain products. They prove successful in changing the way businesses operate, forcing them to consider their environmental footprint and their patterns of production. When social pressure affects their earnings, businesses clearly have to find ways to produce differently. This shows us the great need for a sense of social responsibility on the part of consumers ...

We are always capable of going out of ourselves toward the other. Unless we do this, other creatures will not be recognized for their true worth; we are unconcerned about caring for things for the sake of others; we fail to set limits on ourselves in order to avoid the suffering of others or the deterioration of our surroundings. Disinterested concern for others and the rejection of every form of self-centeredness and self-absorption are essential if we truly wish to care for our brothers and sisters and for the natural environment. These attitudes also attune us to the moral imperative of assessing the impact of our every action and personal decision on the world around us. If we can overcome individualism, we will truly be able to develop a different lifestyle and bring about significant changes in society.

An awareness of the gravity of today's cultural and ecological crisis must be translated into new habits. Many people know that our current progress and the mere amassing of things and pleasures are not enough to give meaning and joy to the human heart, yet they feel unable to give up what the market sets before them. In those countries which should be making the greatest changes in consumer habits, young people have a new ecological sensitivity and a generous spirit, and some of them are making admirable efforts to protect the environment. At the same time, they have grown up in a milieu of extreme consumerism and affluence which makes it difficult to develop other habits. We are faced with an educational challenge.

Environmental education has broadened its goals. Whereas in the beginning it was mainly centered on scientific information, consciousness-raising, and the prevention of environmental risks, it tends now to include a critique of the "myths" of a modernity grounded in a utilitarian mindset (individualism, unlimited progress, competition, consumerism, the unregulated market). It seeks also to restore the various levels of ecological equilibrium, establishing harmony within ourselves, with others, with nature and other living creatures, and with God. Environmental education should facilitate making the leap toward the transcendent which gives ecological ethics its deepest meaning. It needs educators capable of developing an ethics of ecology, and helping people, through effective pedagogy, to grow in solidarity, responsibility, and compassionate care.

Yet this education, aimed at creating an "ecological citizenship," is at times limited to providing information and fails to instill good habits. The existence of laws and regulations is insufficient in the long run to curb bad conduct, even when effective means of enforcement are present. If the laws are to bring about significant, long-lasting effects, the majority of the members of society must be adequately motivated to accept them, and personally transformed to respond. Only by cultivating sound virtues will people be able to make a selfless ecological commitment. A person who could afford to spend and consume more but regularly uses less heating and wears warmer clothes, shows the kind of convictions and attitudes that help to protect the environment. There is a nobility in the duty to care for creation through little daily actions, and it is wonderful how education can bring about real changes in lifestyle. Education in environmental responsibility can encourage ways of acting that directly and significantly affect the world around us, such as avoiding the use of plastic and paper, reducing water consumption, separating refuse, cooking only what can reasonably be consumed, showing care for other living beings, using public transport or car-pooling, planting trees, turning off unnecessary lights, or any number of other practices. All of these reflect a generous and worthy creativity which brings out the best in human beings. Reusing something instead of immediately discarding it, when done for the right reasons, can be an act of love that expresses our own dignity.

We must not think that these efforts are not going to change the world. They benefit society, often unbeknown to us, for they call forth a goodness which, albeit unseen, inevitably tends to spread. Furthermore, such actions can restore our sense of self-esteem; they can enable us to live more fully and to feel that life on earth is worthwhile.

—*Encyclical* Laudato Si', *206–12, May 24, 2015*

ECOLOGICAL CONVERSION

The rich heritage of Christian spirituality, the fruit of twenty centuries of personal and communal experience, has a precious contribution to make to the renewal of humanity. Here, I would like to offer Christians a few suggestions for an ecological spirituality grounded in the convictions of our faith, since the teachings of the gospel have direct consequences for our way of thinking, feeling, and living. More than in ideas or concepts as such, I am interested in how such a spirituality can motivate us to a more passionate concern for the protection of our world. A commitment this lofty cannot be sustained by doctrine alone without a spirituality capable of inspiring us, without an "interior impulse which encourages, motivates, nourishes and gives meaning to our individual and communal activity" (*Evangelii Gaudium*, 261). Admittedly, Christians have not always appropriated and developed the spiritual treasures bestowed by God upon the Church, where the life of the spirit is not dissociated from the body or from nature or from worldly realities, but lived in and with them, in communion with all that surrounds us...

The ecological crisis is also a summons to profound interior conversion. It must be said that some committed and prayerful Christians, with the excuse of realism and pragmatism, tend to ridicule expressions of concern for the environment. Others are passive; they choose not to change their habits and thus become inconsistent. So what they all need is an "ecological conversion," whereby the effects of their encounter with Jesus Christ become evident in their relationship with the world around them. Living our vocation to be protectors of God's handiwork is essential to a life of virtue; it is not an optional or a secondary aspect of our Christian experience.

In calling to mind the figure of Saint Francis of Assisi, we come to realize that a healthy relationship with creation is one dimension of overall personal conversion, which entails the recognition of our errors, sins, faults, and failures, and leads to heartfelt repentance and desire to change...

Nevertheless, self-improvement on the part of individuals will not by itself remedy the extremely complex situation facing our world today. Isolated individuals can lose their ability and freedom to escape the utilitarian mindset, and end up prey to an unethical consumerism bereft of social or ecological awareness. Social problems must be addressed by community networks and not simply by the sum of individual good deeds. This task "will make such tremendous demands of man that he could never achieve it by individual initiative or even by the united effort of men bred in an individualistic way. The work of dominating the world calls for a union of skills and a unity of achievement that can only grow from quite a different attitude" (Romano Guardini, *The End of the Modern World*). The ecological conversion needed to bring about lasting change is also a community conversion.

—*Encyclical* Laudato Si', *206–12, May 24, 2015*

9

Constructing the Human City

God Lives in Our Cities

Living in a big city is not always easy. A multicultural context presents many complex challenges. Yet big cities are a reminder of the hidden riches present in our world: in the diversity of its cultures, traditions, and historical experiences, in the variety of its languages, costumes and cuisine. Big cities bring together all the different ways through which we human beings have discovered to express the meaning of life, wherever we may be.

But big cities also conceal the faces of all those people who don't appear to belong, or are second-class citizens. In big cities, beneath the roar of traffic, beneath "the rapid pace of change," so many faces pass by unnoticed because they have no "right" to be there, no right to be part of the city. They are the foreigners, the children who go without schooling, those deprived of medical insurance, the homeless, the forgotten elderly. These people stand at the edges of our great avenues, in our streets, in deafening anonymity. They become part of an urban landscape that is more and more taken for granted, in our eyes, and especially in our hearts.

Knowing that Jesus still walks our streets, that he is part of the lives of his people, that he is involved with us in one vast history of salvation, fills us with hope. A hope which liberates us from the forces pushing us to isolation and lack of concern for the lives of others, for the life of our city. A hope which frees us from empty "connections," from abstract analyses or sensationalist routines. A hope which is unafraid of involvement, which acts as a leaven wherever we happen to live and work. A hope which makes us see, even in the midst of smog, the presence of God as he continues to walk the streets of our city. Because God is in the city.

What is it like, this light traveling through our streets? How do we encounter God, who lives with us amid the smog of our cities? How do we encounter Jesus, alive and at work in the daily life of our multicultural cities?

The prophet Isaiah can guide us in this process of "learning to see." He speaks of the light which is Jesus. And now he presents Jesus to us as "Wonderful Counselor, the Mighty God, the Everlasting Father, the Prince of Peace." In this way, he introduces us to the life of the Son, so that his life can be our life.

Wonderful Counselor. The gospels tell us how many people came up to Jesus to ask: "Master, what must we do?" The first thing that Jesus does in response is to propose, to encourage, to motivate. He keeps telling his disciples to go, to go out. He urges them to go out and meet others where they really are, not where we think they should be. Go out, again and again, go out without fear, go out without hesitation. Go out and proclaim this joy which is for all the people.

The Mighty God. In Jesus, God himself became Emmanuel, God-with-us, the God who walks alongside us, who gets involved in our lives, in our homes, in the midst of our "pots and pans," as Saint Teresa of Jesus liked to say.

The Everlasting Father. No one and nothing can separate us from his love. Go out and proclaim, go out and show that God is in your midst as a merciful father who himself goes out, morning and evening, to see if his son has returned home and, as soon as he sees him coming, runs out to embrace him. This is beautiful. An embrace that wants to take up, purify, and elevate the dignity of his children. A father who, in his embrace, is "glad tidings to the poor, healing to the afflicted, liberty to captives, comfort to those who mourn" (Is 61:1–2).

Prince of Peace. Go out to others and share the good news that God, our Father, walks at our side. He frees us from anonymity, from a life of emptiness, and brings us to the school of encounter. He removes us from the fray of competition and self-absorption, and he opens before us the path of peace. That peace which is born of accepting others, that peace which fills our hearts whenever we look upon those in need as our brothers and sisters.

God is living in our cities. The Church is living in our cities. God and the Church living in our cities want to be like yeast in the dough, to relate to everyone, to stand at everyone's side, proclaiming the marvels of the Wonderful Counselor, the Mighty God, the Eternal Father, the Prince of Peace.

"The people who walked in darkness have seen a great light." And we, as Christians, are witnesses to this.

—*Homily at Madison Square Garden, New York City, September 25, 2015*

The Defense of Dignity

There is much that we can do to benefit the poor, the needy, and those who suffer, and to favor justice, promote reconciliation, and build peace. But before all else we need to keep alive in our world the thirst for the absolute and to counter the dominance of a one-dimensional vision of the human person, a vision which reduces human beings to what they produce and to what they consume: this is one of the most insidious temptations of our time.

We know how much violence has resulted in recent times from the attempt to eliminate God and the divine from the horizon of humanity, and we are aware of the importance of witnessing in our societies to that primordial openness to transcendence which lies deep within the human heart. In this, we also sense our closeness to all those men and women who, although not identifying themselves as followers of any religious tradition, are nonetheless searching for truth, goodness, and beauty, the truth, goodness, and beauty of God. They are our valued allies in the commitment to defending human dignity in building a peaceful coexistence between peoples and in safeguarding and caring for creation.

—*Address to Representatives of the Churches, Ecclesial Communities, and Other Religions, March 20, 2013*

SERVING THE PERSON, NOT THE IDEOLOGY

Far from any kind of elitism, the horizon to which Jesus points us is not for those few privileged souls capable of attaining the heights of knowledge or different levels of spirituality. The horizon to which Jesus points us always has to do with daily life, also here on "our island," something which can season our daily lives with eternity.

Who is the most important? Jesus is straightforward in his reply: "Whoever wishes to be the first—the most important—among you must be the last of all, and the servant of all." Whoever wishes to be great must serve others, not be served by others.

This is the great paradox of Jesus. The disciples were arguing about who would have the highest place, who would be chosen for privileges—they were the disciples, those closest to Jesus, and they were arguing about that!—who would be above the common law, the general norm, in order to stand out in the quest for superiority over others, who would climb the ladder most quickly to take the jobs that carry certain benefits.

Jesus upsets their "logic," their mindset, simply by telling them that life is lived authentically in a concrete commitment to our neighbor. That is, by serving.

The call to serve involves something special, to which we must be attentive. Serving means caring for [others'] vulnerability, caring for the vulnerable of our families, our society, our people. Theirs are the suffering, fragile, and downcast faces which Jesus tells us specifically to look at and which he asks us to love with a love that takes shape in our actions and decisions. With a love that finds expression in whatever tasks we, as citizens, are called to perform. It is people of flesh and blood, people with individual lives and stories, and with all their frailty, that Jesus asks us to protect, to care for, and to serve. Being a Christian entails promoting the dignity of our brothers and sisters, fighting for it, living for it. That is why Christians are constantly called to set aside their own wishes and desires, their pursuit of power, before the concrete gaze of those who are most vulnerable.

There is a kind of "service" that serves others, yet we need to be careful not to be tempted by another kind of service, one that is "self-serving" with regard to others. There is a way to go about serving that is interested in only helping "my people," "our people." This service always leaves "your people" outside, and gives rise to a process of exclusion.

All of us are called by virtue of our Christian vocation to that service which truly serves, and to help one another not to be tempted by a "service" that is really "self-serving." All of us are asked, indeed urged, by Jesus to care for one another out of love, without looking to one side or the other to see what our neighbor is doing or not doing. Jesus says: "Whoever would be first among you must be the last, and the servant of all." That person will be the first. Jesus does not say: If your neighbor wants to be first, let him be the servant! We have to be careful to avoid judgmental looks and renew our belief in the transforming look to which Jesus invites us.

This caring for others out of love is not about being servile. Rather, it means putting the question of our brothers and sisters at the center. Service always looks to their faces, touches their flesh, senses their closeness, and even, in some cases, "suffers" that closeness and tries to help them. Service is never ideological, for we do not serve ideas, we serve people.

—*Homily in Havana, Cuba, September 20, 2015*

TOUCHING HUMAN MISERY

Jesus' sacrifice on the cross is nothing else than the culmination of the way he lived his entire life. Moved by his example, we want to enter fully into the fabric of society, sharing the lives of all, listening to their concerns, helping them materially and spiritually in their needs, rejoicing with those who rejoice, weeping with those who weep. Arm in arm with others, we are committed to building a new world. But we do so not from a sense of obligation, not as a burdensome duty, but as the result of a personal decision that brings us joy and gives meaning to our lives.

Sometimes we are tempted to be that kind of Christian who keeps the Lord's wounds at arm's length. Yet Jesus wants us to touch human misery, to touch the suffering flesh of others. He hopes that we will stop looking for those personal or communal niches that shelter us from the maelstrom of human misfortune and instead enter into the reality of other people's lives and know the power of tenderness. Whenever we do so, our lives become wonderfully complicated and we experience intensely what it is to be a people, to be part of a people.

—*Apostolic Exhortation* Evangelii Gaudium, *269–70, November 24, 2013*

Poverty Teaches Solidarity

Poverty teaches solidarity, sharing, and charity, and is also expressed in moderation and joy in the essential, to put us on guard against material idols that obscure the real meaning of life. A poverty learned with the humble, the poor, the sick, and all those who are on the existential outskirts of life. A theoretical poverty is no use to us. Poverty is learned by touching the flesh of the poor Christ, in the humble, in the poor, in the sick, and in children.

—Address to the Union of Superiors General, May 8, 2013

THE RESPONSIBILITY OF BELIEVERS

Any technical solution that science claims to offer will be powerless to solve the serious problems of our world if humanity loses its compass, if we lose sight of the great motivations that make it possible for us to live in harmony, to make sacrifices, and to treat others well. Believers themselves must constantly feel challenged to live in a way consonant with their faith and not to contradict it by their actions. They need to be encouraged to be ever open to God's grace and to draw constantly from their deepest convictions about love, justice, and peace.

If a mistaken understanding of our own principles has at times led us to justify mistreating nature, to exercise tyranny over creation, to engage in war, injustice, and acts of violence, we believers should acknowledge that by so doing we were not faithful to the treasures of wisdom which we have been called to protect and preserve.

Cultural limitations in different eras often affected the perception of these ethical and spiritual treasures, yet by constantly returning to their sources, religions will be better equipped to respond to today's needs.

—Encyclical Laudato Si', 200, May 24, 2015

WE NEED EACH OTHER

Care for nature is part of a lifestyle that includes the capacity for living together and communion. Jesus reminded us that we have God as our common Father and that this makes us brothers and sisters. Fraternal love can only be gratuitous; it can never be a means of repaying others for what they have done or will do for us. That is why it is possible to love our enemies. This same gratuitousness inspires us to love and accept the wind, the sun, and the clouds, even though we cannot control them...

We must regain the conviction that we need one another, that we have a shared responsibility for others and the world, and that being good and decent are worth it. We have had enough of immorality and the mockery of ethics, goodness, faith, and honesty. It is time to acknowledge that light-hearted superficiality has done us no good. When the foundations of social life are corroded, what ensues are battles over conflicting interests, new forms of violence and brutality, and obstacles to the growth of a genuine culture of care for the environment.

—*Encyclical* Laudato Si', *228–29, May 24, 2015*

UNIVERSAL FRATERNITY

The common home of all men and women must continue to rise on the foundations of a right understanding of universal fraternity and respect for the sacredness of every human life, of every man and every woman, the poor, the elderly, children, the infirm, the unborn, the unemployed, the abandoned, those considered disposable because they are considered only as part of a statistic. This common home of all men and women must also be built on the understanding of a certain sacredness of created nature.

Such understanding and respect call for a higher degree of wisdom, one that accepts transcendence, self-transcendence, rejects the creation of an all-powerful élite, and recognizes that the full meaning of individual and collective life is found in selfless service to others and in the wise and respectful use of creation for the common good. To repeat the words of Paul VI, "the edifice of modern civilization has to be built on spiritual principles, for they are the only ones capable not only of supporting it but of shedding light on it" (Speech to Representatives of the States, October 4, 1965).

El Gaucho Martín Fierro, a classic piece of literature from my native land, says: "Brothers should stand by each other, because this is the first law; keep a true bond between you always, at all times—because if you fight among yourselves, you'll be devoured by those outside."

The contemporary world, so apparently connected, is experiencing a growing and steady social fragmentation, which places at risk "the foundations of social life" and consequently leads to "battles over conflicting interests" (*Laudato Si'*, 229).

The present time invites us to give priority to actions that generate new processes in society, so as to bear fruit in significant and positive historical events (cf. *Evangelii Gaudium*, 223). We cannot permit ourselves to postpone "certain agendas" for the future. The future demands of us critical and global decisions in the face of world-wide conflicts which increase the number of the excluded and those in need.

—Address to the General Assembly of the United Nations,
New York, September 25, 2015

10

The Spiritual Dimension of Life

The great danger in today's world, pervaded as it is by consumerism, is the desolation, the anguish born of a complacent yet covetous heart, the feverish pursuit of frivolous pleasures, and a blunted conscience.

Whenever our interior life becomes caught up in its own interests and concerns, there is no longer room for others, no place for the poor. God's voice is no longer heard, the quiet joy of his love is no longer felt, and the desire to do good fades. This is a very real danger for believers too. Many fall prey to it, and end up resentful, angry, and listless.

That is no way to live a dignified and fulfilled life; it is not God's will for us, nor is it the life in the Spirit which has its source in the heart of the risen Christ.

—*Apostolic Exhortation*, Evangelii Gaudium, 2, *November 24, 2013*

QUALITY OF LIFE

Christian spirituality proposes an alternative understanding of the quality of life, and encourages a prophetic and contemplative lifestyle, one capable of deep enjoyment free of the obsession with consumption. We need to take up an ancient lesson, found in different religious traditions and also in the Bible. It is the conviction that "less is more." A constant flood of new consumer goods can baffle the heart and prevent us from cherishing each thing and each moment. To be serenely present to each reality, however small it may be, opens us to much greater horizons of understanding and personal fulfilment. Christian spirituality proposes a growth marked by moderation and the capacity to be happy with little. It is a return to that simplicity which allows us to stop and appreciate the small things, to be grateful for the opportunities which life affords us, to be spiritually detached from what we possess, and not to succumb to sadness for what we lack. This implies avoiding the dynamic of dominion and the mere accumulation of pleasures.

—*Encyclical* Laudato Si', 222, *May 24, 2015*

SHARING WITH OTHERS

Jesus frequently warned the rich, because they greatly risk placing their security in the goods of this world, and security, the final security, is in God. In a heart possessed by wealth there isn't much room for faith: everything is involved with wealth, there is no room for faith. If, however, one gives God his rightful place, that is first place, then his love leads one to share even one's wealth, to set it at the service of projects of solidarity and development, as so many examples demonstrate, even recent ones, in the history of the Church. And in this way God's providence comes through our service to others, our sharing with others. If each of us accumulates not for ourselves alone but for the service of others, in this case, in this act of solidarity, the providence of God is made visible. If, however, one accumulates only for oneself, what will happen when one is called by God? No one can take his riches with him, because—as you know—the shroud has no pockets! It is better to share, for we can take with us to heaven only what we have shared with others.

—*Angelus Prayer, March 2, 2014*

WELCOMING OTHERS

Jesus calls his disciples and sends them out, giving them clear and precise instructions. He challenges them to take on a whole range of attitudes and ways of acting. Sometimes these can strike us as exaggerated or even absurd. It would be easier to interpret these attitudes symbolically or "spiritually." But Jesus is quite precise, very clear. He doesn't tell them simply to do whatever they think they can.

Let us think about some of these attitudes: "Take nothing for the journey except a staff; no bread, no bag, no money..." "When you enter a house, stay there until you leave the place" (cf. Mk 6:8-11). All this might seem quite unrealistic.

We could concentrate on the words, "bread," "money," "bag," "staff," "sandals," and "tunic." And this would be fine. But it strikes me that one key word can easily pass unnoticed among the challenging words I have just listed. It is a word at the heart of Christian spirituality, of our experience of discipleship: "welcome." Jesus as the good master, the good teacher, sends them out to be welcomed, to experience hospitality. He says to them: "Where you enter a house, stay there." He sends them out to learn one of the hallmarks of the community of believers. We might say that a Christian is someone who has learned to welcome others, who has learned to show hospitality.

—*Homily in Asunción, Paraguay, July 12, 2015*

HEALING FUNDAMENTAL RELATIONSHIPS

The critique of a misguided anthropocentrism must not underestimate the importance of interpersonal relations. If the present ecological crisis is one small sign of the ethical, cultural, and spiritual crisis of modernity, we cannot presume to heal our relationship with nature and the environment without healing all fundamental human relationships.

Christian thought sees human beings as possessing a particular dignity above other creatures; it thus inculcates esteem for each person and respect for others. Our openness to others, each of whom is a "thou" capable of knowing, loving, and entering into dialogue, remains the source of our nobility as human persons.

A correct relationship with the created world demands that we not weaken this social dimension of openness to others, much less the transcendent dimension of our openness to the "Thou" of God. Our relationship with the environment can never be isolated from our relationship with others and with God. Otherwise, it would be nothing more than romantic individualism dressed up in ecological garb, locking us into a stifling immanence.

—*Encyclical* Laudato Si', *119, May 24, 2015*

KEEPING HOPE ALIVE

Hope speaks to us of something deeply rooted in every human heart, independent of our concrete circumstances and historical conditioning. Hope speaks to us of a thirst, an aspiration, a longing for a life of fulfillment, a desire to achieve great things, things which fill our heart and lift our spirit to lofty realities like truth, goodness and beauty, justice and love. But it also involves taking risks. It means being ready not to be seduced by what is fleeting, by false promises of happiness, by immediate and selfish pleasures, by a life of mediocrity and self-centeredness, which only fills the heart with sadness and bitterness. No, hope is bold; it can look beyond personal convenience, the petty securities and compensations that limit our horizon, and can open us up to grand ideals that make life more beautiful and worthwhile...

How do we find paths of hope in the situations in which we live? How do we make those hopes for fulfillment, authenticity, justice, and truth become a reality in our personal lives, in our country, and our world? I think that there are three ideas that can help to keep our hope alive:

Hope is a path made of memory and discernment. Hope is the virtue which goes places. It isn't simply a path we take for the pleasure of it, but it has an end, a goal that is practical and lights up our way. Hope is also nourished by memory; it looks not only to the future but also to the past and present. To keep moving forward in life, in addition to knowing where we want to go, we also need to know who we are and where we come from. Individuals or peoples who have no memory and erase their past risk losing their identity and destroying their future. So we need to remember who we are, and in what our spiritual and moral heritage consists. This, I believe, was the experience and the insight of that great Cuban, Father Félix Varela. Discernment is also needed, because it is essential to be open to reality and to be able to interpret it without fear or prejudice. Partial and ideological interpretations are useless; they only disfigure reality by trying to fit it into our preconceived schemas, and they always cause disappointment and despair. We need discernment and memory, because discernment is not blind; it is built on solid ethical and moral criteria which help us to see what is good and just.

Hope is a path taken with others. An African proverb says: "If you want to go fast, go alone; if you want to go far, go with others." Isolation and aloofness never generate hope; but closeness to others and encounter do. Left to ourselves, we will go nowhere. Nor by exclusion will we be able to build a future for anyone, even ourselves. A path of hope calls for a culture of encounter and dialogue, which can overcome conflict and sterile confrontation. To create that culture, it is vital to see different ways of thinking not in terms of risk, but of richness and growth. The world needs this culture of encounter. It needs young people who seek to know and love one another, to journey together in building a country like that which José Martí dreamed of: "With all, and for the good of all."

Hope is a path of solidarity. The culture of encounter should naturally lead to a culture of solidarity...Without solidarity, no country has a future. Beyond all other considerations or interests, there has to be concern for that person who may be my friend, my companion, but also someone who may think differently from the way I do, someone with his own ideas yet just as human and just as Cuban as I am. Simple tolerance is not enough; we have to go well beyond that, passing from a suspicious and defensive attitude to one of acceptance, cooperation, concrete service, and effective assistance. Do not be afraid of solidarity, service, and offering a helping hand, so that no one is excluded from the path.

This path of life is lit up by a higher hope: the hope born of our faith in Christ. He made himself our companion along the way. Not only does he encourage us, he also accompanies us; he is at our side and he extends a friendly hand to us. The Son of God, he wanted to become someone like us, to accompany us on our way. Faith in his presence, in his friendship and love, lights up all our hopes and dreams. With him at our side, we learn to discern what is real, to encounter and serve others, and to walk the path of solidarity.

—*Address to Students at the Fr. Félix Varela Cultural Center,*
Havana, September 20, 2015

A REVOLUTION OF TENDERNESS

The gospel reading about the Annunciation (Lk 1:26–28) tells us about something the Lord does every time he visits us: he calls us out of our house. These are images which we are asked to contemplate over and over again. God's presence in our lives never leaves us tranquil: it always pushes to do something. When God comes, he always calls us out of our house. We are visited so that we can visit others; we are encountered so as to encounter others; we receive love in order to give love.

In the gospel we see Mary, the first disciple, a young woman of perhaps between fifteen and seventeen years of age who, in a small village of Palestine, was visited by the Lord who told her that she was to be the mother of the Savior. Mary was far from "thinking it was all about her," or thinking that everyone had to come and wait upon her. She left her house and went out to serve. First she goes to help her cousin Elizabeth. The joy that blossoms when we know that God is with us, with our people, gets our heart beating, gets our legs moving and "draws us out of ourselves." It leads us to take the joy we have received and to share it in service, in those "pregnant" situations which our neighbors or families may be experiencing. The gospel tells us that Mary went in haste, slowly but surely, with a steady pace, neither too fast nor so slow as never to get there. Neither anxious nor distracted, Mary goes with haste to accompany her cousin who has conceived in her old age. Henceforth this was always to be her way. She has always been the woman who visits men and women, children, the elderly, and the young. She has visited and accompanied many of our people in the drama of their birth. She has watched over the struggles of those who fought to defend the rights of their children. And now, she continues to bring us the Word of Life, her Son, our Lord . . .

"Whenever we look to Mary, we come to believe once again in the revolutionary nature of love and tenderness" (*Evangelii Gaudium*, 288).

Generation after generation, day after day, we are asked to renew our faith. We are asked to live the revolution of tenderness as Mary, our Mother of Charity, did. We are invited to "leave home" and to open our eyes and hearts to others. Our revolution comes about through tenderness, through the joy which always becomes closeness and compassion—which is not pity, but suffering with, so as to free—and leads us to get involved in, and to serve, the life of others. Our faith makes us leave our homes and go forth to encounter others, to share their joys, their hopes, and their frustrations. Our faith, "calls us out of our house," to visit the sick, the prisoner, and to those who mourn. It makes us able to laugh with those who laugh and rejoice with our neighbors who rejoice. Like Mary, we want to be a Church which serves, which leaves home and goes forth, which goes forth from its chapels, forth from its sacristies, in order to accompany life, to sustain hope, to be the sign of unity of a noble and worthy people. Like Mary, Mother of Charity, we want to be a Church which goes forth to build bridges, to break down walls, to sow seeds of reconciliation.

—*Mass at the Shrine of the "Virgen de la Caridad de Cobre,"*
Santiago de Cuba, September 22, 2015